A division of LUMMOX Press

THE LIBERAL MEDIA MADE ME DO IT!

Poems Inspired by Stories on PBS & NPR

Edited by Robbi Nester

©2014 by Robbi Nester

All rights reserved. No part of this book may be reproduced without the express written permission of the author, except in the case of written reviews.

ISBN 978-1-929878-72-7

First edition

A division of LUMMOX Press
PO Box 5301
San Pedro, CA 90733
www.lummoxpress.com/lc/

Printed in the United States of America

Acknowledgement

Thanks to Lavina Blossom for being such a stalwart reader and assistant editor, the voice of reason when I lost perspective. Thanks also to Mary Bullington for offering both her writing and artwork, Chris Yeseta for cover and layout, and of course, thank you to RD Armstrong, without whom this volume would not have been possible. Finally, lest I forget, thank you to all of you who submitted poems, whether they ended up in the final volume or not.

Table of Contents

Introduction   Robbi Nester   —xi
What Unites Us   RD Armstrong   —xii
About My Process   Robbi Nester   —xiii

Poems with asterisks* have links to source stories in the back of the book.

THE NEWS

The Bird World   Howie Good*   —3
Technophobia   Howie Good*   —4
The News Hour   Mary Boxley Bullington   —5
Listening to the News in Creole on NPR
    Barbra Nightingale   —6
All Things Considered   Ron. Lavalette   —7
Quietly Getting Smart   Robin Stratton   —8
NPR Report: 200 Elephants Slaughtered in Cameroon
    Susan Snowden   —9
Ashes   Kenneth Hart   —10
Unenforceable   Robbi Nester   —11
The Wiretappers Ball   Deborah Gang*   —12
Great Fires   Onna Solomon*   —13
Just You Wait   Juleigh Howard-Hobson*   —14
Poem After the Nightly Business Report
    Michael Colonnese   —15
Contrast   Hal O'Leary   —16
Blame   Hal O' Leary   —17
Into a Void: A Found Poem   M.E. Hope*   —18
What Happens   Judy Kronenfeld   —20
High-Water Mark   Deda Kavanagh   —22
Something About Crickets   RD Armstrong   —23
Boy   Luisa A. Igloria*   —24

SCIENCE

Cold Front in Miami *Barbra Nightingale* —27
The Weight of It All *Barbra Nightingale* —28
Dark Matter *Lisa Gluskin Stonestreet* —29
All Bacteria Considered *Kelly Nelson** —30
Fistulated Cow *Robbi Nester** —32
Exchange *Robbi Nester** —34
Limulus Polyphemus *Kathryn Kopple** —36
Mute *Anne Baber* —38
Eating in Winter *Barbara Duffey** —40
Radio Lab: **Space** *Kris Bigalk* —41
USDA Drops Poison on Guam *Patricia Scruggs* —43
Leaf-Cutter Ants *Richard Nester* —44
The Trees and the Vines *Tim Kahl** —45

PEOPLE

Radio Lab: **Scientist** *Kris Bigalk* —49
Seeing *Kris Bigalk* —50
The Forest of Her *Christina Lovin* —51
Comatose *Kris Bigalk* —53
Living Will *Kris Bigalk* —54
Like the Wings of the Butterfly *RD Armstrong* —56
Writing Blindly *Christina Lovin** —57
A Cup of White Sugar *Christina Lovin* —59
Textile *Luisa A. Igloria* —61
pulled blinds *Kit Zak* —62
SWS-87: The Voice of Rachel *Martha O. Adams* —63

Table of Contents *(continued)*

Thinning *Amy MacLennan** —66
My Brother's Wandering Soul *Brittney Scott** —68
His Eye *Penelope Scrambly Schott* —70
Her Education *Meryl Stratford* —71
Sonnets For the Lost and Surviving *Kirstin Bratt** —72
After a Testimony by Usman Farman *Robbi Nester* —74
The Last Days of the Balkh Bastan *M.E. Silverman* —76
The Herdsman & the Dolphin *M.E. Silverman* —78
André Trocmé *Marly Youmans* —79
The Three Dreams of Karl Henize *Sheryl Clough* —80
Remembering Blossom Dearie *Nina Soifer* —82
House of Poems *Donna Decker* —83

EPIPHANIES

Now I am Nothing *RD Armstrong* —87
Happiness *Robbi Nester* —89
Poem on a Line by Anne Sexton *Barbara Crooker* —90
The Stock Market Loses Fluidity *Barbara Crooker* —91
Lucy *Joan Mazza** —92
Radio Interview *Marie Kane* —93
A Retired Athlete *Richard Hamwi* —94
Aubade With a Quincy Jones Biography on PBS
    Barbara Duffey —96
In the Depths of the Recession *Rupert Fike* —98
Pale Blue Dot *Martha Silano* —99
To Be Continued *Robbi Nester* —101
The Inheritors *Lavina Blossom** —103

ETCETERA

Strap a Tikker on Your Wrist, Stretch Your Arm to Heaven
    Kate Hutchinson* —107
Near Misses *Barbra Nightingale* —109
The Bats of Carlsbad Caverns Ponder Their Ancestors
    Barbara Duffey* —110
Making Whole Hive Mead *Robbi Nester* —111
Roast Suckling Pig *Judy Kronenfeld* —112
The Foundling Wheel *Blas Falconer* —113
Dead Air *Julie Bruck* —115
Belonging *Jennifer Flescher* —116
***Radio Lab:* Colors** *Kris Bigalk* —117
Folklore: Practice and Theory
    Jane Rosenberg LaForge* —118
Staccato *Susan Blackwell Ramsey** —119
Three Public Radio Haikus *Elizabeth Kerlikowske* —120
Proofs *Sally Ball* —121
Candlestick Patterns *Amy MacLennan** —122
Fire *Robbi Nester* —124
Revision *Allen Braden* —125
Tell Me If You've Heard This One
    Susan Blackwell Ramsey —126

Sources for the Poems —128

Contributors —132

Introduction

WITH ALL THE MANY FORMS of entertainment and distraction open to us, National Public Radio and television may be the ones most favored by writers.

The quiet confiding voice of radio sees us through our commutes, educates, and amuses us. We feel that we know the hosts on such shows as *All Things Considered, RadioLab, This American Life, Prairie Home Companion, Snap Judgment,* and that they could be friends, sharing our interests and sensibilities.

Their voices accompany us as we go about our daily business, and they are there for us again when we return home, welcoming us with news of what has unfolded while we were otherwise occupied.

For its part, Public television becomes a trusted sanctuary from crass commercials, laugh tracks, unfunny comedies rising in volume as they grow more empty in content. We start with shows like *Sesame Street, Electric Company, Mr. Rogers, Reading Rainbow* and continue on to *Frontline, The Nightly News,* and the many guilty pleasures of adult Anglophiles, such as *Masterpiece Theater* and *Mystery.*

It shouldn't surprise us then to see that so many have responded in kind, speaking back to the speakers, inspired by what they hear and see. What may be more surprising is that no one seems to have had the idea of gathering these works together into an anthology before, though they have appeared here and there, in poetry collections and journals.

For me, the greatest delight in receiving these pieces has been to recognize the stories I have heard and seen before, with another's perception added in. This brings home the truth that each of us could start with the same raw material and yet produce finished products that resemble one another only in incidental ways.

Our national tragedies and triumphs, the odd idiosyncratic stories of individuals, the stuff of our daily lives and explorations all appear here, care of the diligent reporters of our national media.

It is wonderful to realize that in some sense we are all one, listening or watching alone in the dark, but part of a larger tribe. This may be the closest thing we can experience to unanimity and belonging in this fractured land.

Robbi Nester
Editor

This poem was inspired by a documentary on PBS about a man in Iraq who runs a generator to supply electricity to his part of Baghdad. At one point, he and a friend are sitting in a cafe playing dominoes and drinking coffee and he says something to the effect that they have to do this every day in order to remain sane, because being the electricity guy is pretty thankless and his life is pretty chaotic. He just wants to think that his life matters.

What Unites Us

The need to feel like
You are a human being
Is universal
Whether you are trying
To make ends meet
In Baghdad
Tehran
Haifa
Basra
Tripoli
Paris
Belfast
Detroit
South Central
Birmingham
West Oakland
Riverside
Or even Long Beach

That is what unites us
This longing to be treated
As if our lives matter

RD Armstrong

About My Process

IN CHOOSING THE POEMS for this anthology, I had a few basic guidelines in mind: the poems should be inspired by a specific show or episode of a show aired on public media (I very soon realized that NPR and PBS alone did not cover all of these), and should probably not be mere iterations of a general news story treated on multiple media, unless the treatment the story received was exceptional or unusual in some way that was reflected in the poem.

I also hoped the authors could write me a summary of the story, giving information about the station and show they heard it on. However, at the same time, I realized that might not be possible in all cases, since I myself could not locate the sources of at least one of my own poems that had its genesis in an NPR story. Normally, after all, the source isn't as important as the poem that emerges from it.

But ultimately, the quality of the poems had to be my top priority, and the way they worked with the other poems I had already accepted.

I knew I wanted a balance of tones, styles, moods, forms, and subject matter. So that is what I sought. And when, as it did in a few cases, that meant I ended up ultimately violating my own rules and accepting poems that lacked a clear source but were the product of a story on public media, according to the writers, I took those because they worked well with the other work and on their own.

The anthology filled up faster than I expected. Though for a while I doubted that I would have sufficient work to make a substantial book, it came in, a little every day.

Maybe this book will inspire others to collect poems from this source. There certainly are a lot of them out there, as I can testify! And for those of you who didn't make it in this time, there are always those future endeavors to look forward to.

Robbi Nester

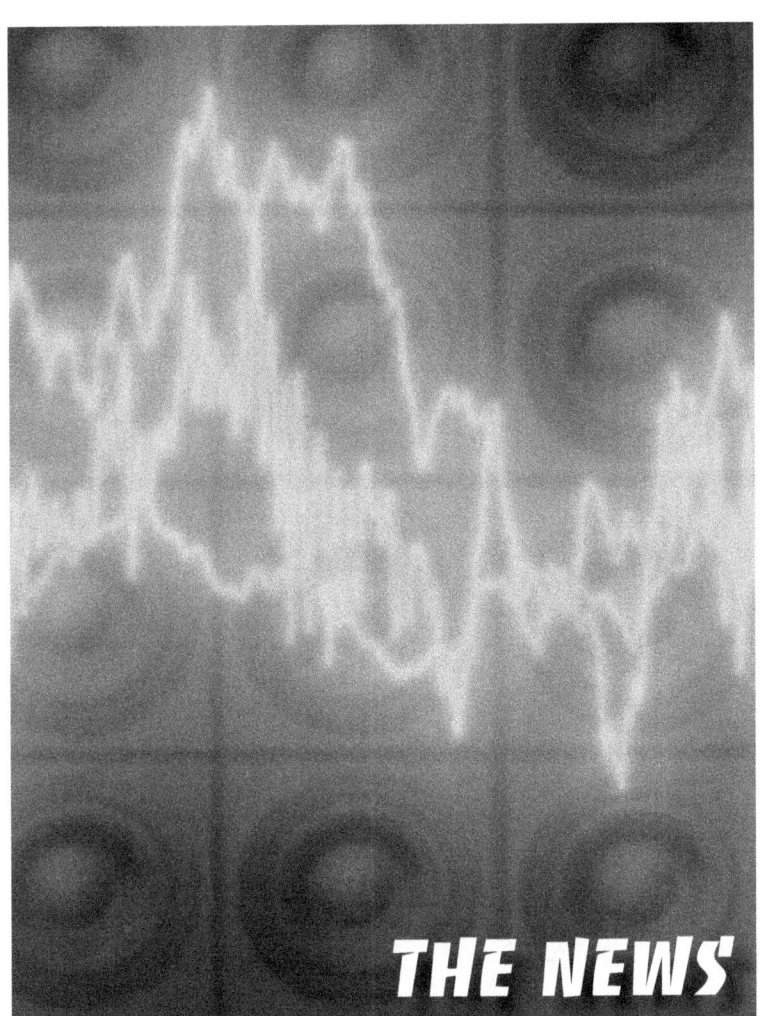

Source: "Birds Of A Feather Spy Together," All Things Considered, *Oct. 13, 2013*

The Bird World

Two men
in a chilly apartment
converse
in whispers.

Little do
they know,
the raven
outside
their window

is not merely
a city scavenger,
but a spy,
kind of Jason Bourne.

Pigeons aren't
that clever.
Owls are not
very smart either.

They may be wise,
but they aren't
particularly smart.

Yes, it's possible
there are still
rogue ravens
flittering around
Eastern Europe

waiting to be
activated.

Howie Good

"Technophobia" springs from the endless news of endless wars being fought here, there, and everywhere (Syria, Afghanistan, etc.), as well as from the increasing Googlization of American society. The latter is something I think about a lot as a journalism professor. The digital revolution is actually the primary topic of one of the courses I teach. I keep a number of NPR pieces with it on tap on my class blog.

Technophobia

They say the day is coming –
and pretty soon, too –
when the souls of the dead
will be uploaded to the Google Cloud,
and God, if He even still exists,
will be able to rest,
drenched in dire purple
and reclining on plush snow,
until needed as an excuse
in whatever year of whatever war.

Howie Good

The News Hour

How calmly they present the latest calamity.
You have to admire
their plain-spoken questions
and tasteful attire

as the ocean rolls into startled
coastal cities, lifts buildings and parked
cars out of their dry-dock moorings
and sets them at war.

In the small New England town
where slain children and teachers
are named in bold type,
television is now the floodlit stage

where the teen-aged gunman,
dressed to kill, hands out
diplomas and final rewards.
We cannot

blame the journalists.
When the news and the weather
bind together our gravest concerns,
our kin and our kind

naturally turn trade to become
our professional mourners,
practiced like us, in labor and love
and dignified keening.

Mary Boxley Bullington

I listen to the news in Creole every night for 15 minutes on WLRN-Miami. I am such an NPR addict (or so lazy) that I never change the channel when the 15 minutes of School board news comes on in Creole for our Haitian population. I don't understand any French (let alone Creole), but I love the sound of the words, and the sprinkling of English throughout.

Listening to the News in Creole on NPR

I don't speak French and certainly not Creole,
and I don't live in Miami-Dade County.
I'm just this white woman advancing
off to the right of middle in age.
But when that lilting junkanoo music
announces the "news in Creole"
I am transfixed, listening to my one
impossible language, the one my mouth
simply will not pronounce, the juicy
diphthongs and vowels, consonants
popping on the tongue, smiling
incomprehensibly, sound without sense.
I find myself playing a game:
how many words do I know?
Waiting for the English thrown in like crumbs
on apple pie: "blue jeans," "tank top." "PTA"
the English they have no words for in French, the words
they've adopted with pride in their place, reaching out,
adapting, becoming Floridian, in the good old "U.S. of A."

Barbra Nightingale

The Liberal Media Made Me Do It

I spend a lot of time behind the wheel, radio almost always tuned to Vermont Public Radio, my hands rarely free to stop and take notes about individual episodes of one of my favorite programs. This poem reflects how several (many) episodes can coalesce for a weary but attentive commuter.

Depending upon which side of Vermont's Green Mountains I'm driving on, I am listening to either WVPA in St Johnsbury or to WVPS in Burlington.

All Things Considered

Three soon-to-be grads from Harvard
or Sarah Lawrence opine on the morning
news how their Senior classes seem
simultaneously base and baseless
in light of their last three years abroad,
considering how, after all, once you've seen
morning in Jalalabad, everything golden
in the heart of the desert, everything wan
and wavering in the high desert heat,
everything else pales by comparison.
Or so they say, three young women
taking their last few classes, studying
The Modern Islamic Middle East, The History
Of Moorish Art, The Economics and Politics
Of Oil Producing Emirates As Reported In
The Western Press, Such As It Is.
One of them has perfect parents in
Prague, will go to live with them as soon as
the mortarboard is tossed in the air;
one of them is hoping for a career in
diplomacy, if she survives a military stint
and a battle for the civil servant's desk.
The third is planning a family
just outside The Beltway, her most
immediate goal a gallery, small showings
on alternate Tuesdays, her house
only a mile or two away, jogging
distance, close enough to push a stroller
or walk a border collie, far enough away
to kid herself she's got a life that matters.

Ron.Lavalette

Quietly Getting Smart

More and more I have been
quietly getting smart
listening to NPR on the radio
of Mom's car
which I am borrowing

I am on top of all the
latest news stories
have many informed opinions
and do well on their weekly
quiz show.

However, sometimes
I want to hear music
So I grab a CD to play
on my way to work
REO Speedwagon

I slip the CD into the slot
Turn up the volume, ready to rock!
But despite my best efforts, no sound emits
And I can't figure out how to make it happen
Not so smart after all.

Robin Stratton

I heard this story on a morning newscast on my local NPR station, WCQS in Asheville, NC. 88.1 FM

National Public Radio Report:
Two Hundred Elephants Slaughtered in Cameroon

I am driving to work
a world away when I hear it,
yet I see that sweltering plain:
shimmering layers of color,
burnt umber, sage, yellow-gold,
the breast of the land
rising and falling,
the relentless sun overhead.

I picture the carcasses rotting:
mothers toppled on calves,
gaping tusk sockets
caked with black blood,
flies moving together,
shrouding the scourge.

Thich Nat Hahn
calls for compassion;
Bishop Tutu
preaches forgiveness.
But today a dark part of me argues.
I want to round up men,
fly to the Ivory Coast
and rout out the poachers,
pin them down and pry out their teeth,
one by one, slowly, slowly.

Susan Snowden
—*Previously published by Victoria Press (Asheville, NC)
   in their 2005 anthology*

The Liberal Media Made Me Do It

The story was a news report back in 2002, most likely on All Things Considered. *It had been discovered that the Tri-State Crematory in Noble, GA had been stashing corpses in the woods surrounding the crematory instead of cremating them. The owner was sentenced to 12 years in prison. His motives were unclear, but it was possible that the incinerator may not have been working properly. The story stated that Tri-State was giving relatives wood ash, rather than remains of the dearly departed.*

Ashes

So it turns out grandma wasn't really grandma
but an oak log, or some pine chips,

now that they found out the crematorium wasn't burning
the bodies it received, but piling them up, in white bags,

which reporters say you could see from an airplane, there were so many.

And now Grandma, Dad, little Christina whom Hodgkin's took:
we paid pilots to fly us over the ocean, we recited death poems

and psalms, we cried and spoke to the golden urns on our bureaus
full of sawdust. And all the while, you were feeling the weight of the others

pressing down on you in the pile. Not even the maggots
could get in to greet you.

There's an ancient story of a woman so loved by a god
he chased her through the forest until she turned into a tree.

Now that was an afterlife.

Kenneth Hart

This poem springs from an interview I heard on The World, *a BBC show aired on NPR, concerning the Turkish government's recent efforts to bend language to its will. Out of puritanism, the heretofore secular government was endeavoring to ban the use of common words in English and Turkish, words such as the ones I mention in the poem.*

Unenforceable

After an interview on BBC's *The World*, aired on NPR
In Istanbul, "forbidden" is forbidden.
For censors in that city, words
are things and things are dangerous:
"canals" conceal back passageways.
"Hot" and "teens" are banished,
yet children still grow older,
summer still persists.

Though words for that or this
may disappear, the body speaks in code,
communicates what custom can't deny.
Censors and lexicographers despair:
"forbidden" makes its home in all the tender
folds between the fingers, no matter that
in Istanbul, "forbidden" is forbidden.

Robbi Nester

This poem had many inspirations including:
NPR Morning Edition 6/13/13 on the NSA's Utah Data Center
and an NPR The Two-Way interview with Snowden.

The Wiretappers Ball

An FBI internet surveillance unit will collaborate with the coming NSA data center in Utah to decipher and monitor email between private citizens. Homeland Security recently began to monitor social media using version 2.1.3 key words & search terms.

Some are obvious. Do not use assassination,
Taliban, bomb, bomb squad, bomb threat.

Al Qaeda (all spellings). But electric? Blackout.
Metro. Power. Smart? Is it worth the risk to say

failure? Dock. Airport. Airplane and its derivatives.
Cancelled. Delays. Hail. Snow. Blizzard.

Why, these are some of your necessary words—
everyone's necessary words. If you suffer blizzards

you need to talk about them and if you don't, you
need to gloat. Wildfire. Ice. Stranded. Stuck.

Temblor. All suspect. Use sleet at your own risk
along with plague. Plume. Enriched. Collapse.

They have marked the best words as hazardous.
Including hazardous. Breach. Mudslide. Grid. San Diego!

Say goodbye to relief and closure. And cyber terror.
Cyber terror is not to be used.   Warning

is on the list.

Deborah Gang

The Liberal Media Made Me Do It

I read this story on the NPR blog The Two-way *in January of 2011.*

Great Fires

On any day you might
in response to the madness that is
your or someone else's government
choose a spot in the public square
amid traffic and mothers at the Saturday market
who chastise children for bruising fruit
amid bicycles and news stands
to light yourself aflame.

It has become tradition: self-immolation
the papers say *spreads like a disease*
(avoiding the obvious morbid simile)—
you have seen the footage of the monk
who sits so still engulfed in the fire of every day
or the fruit seller, an ordinary man, consumed
when a girl is shot for wearing lipstick.

People might lean from their windows
they will certainly recoil from the smell
and may not sleep for the sight of you
still or writhing, dead or saved
and when the news reports on your life
people will know the details of your days—
your job your wife—and they will know
who is capable of such acts.

Onna Solomon

The Liberal Media Made Me Do It

This sonnet was inspired by listening to NPR business news, right before Thanksgiving 2012 on KOPB—Oregon Public Broadcasting.

Just You Wait

While we wait, we keep falling down again...
Pushing deep, deeper, deepest into debt,
Over limits, past due accounts that strain
Against rock bottom (haven't touched it yet
But it's been really close). We need a way
To hold on until we can earn a few
Bucks, to keep our student-loans at bay,
And to pay our lousy credit cards, too.
When things are back to normal, most banks should
Raise our limits or approve more cards. If
We don't go bankrupt on them—if we're good
At reaffirming, if we don't downshift
Once the economy recovers, great
Things will happen for us. If we can wait.

Juleigh Howard-Hobson

The Liberal Media Made Me Do It

The poem wasn't written in response to any specific broadcast, but I do watch the Nightly Business Report at least once a week on UNCTV, where it airs each week-night at 7 PM, right after the News Hour *(PBS).*

I'm functionally illiterate when it comes to business or economics, but as discourse goes, the "experts" in such fields do say some amazing stuff, and it's like listening to Martians who happen to speak English.

Poem After the Nightly Business Report

Long on the rumor.
Short on the news.
If commodities seem robust
and unemployment falls,
that's good news for builders
but fatal for new offerings.
Optimistic projections
could easily inflate prospects,
but too quick a move
could trigger a reversal.
Pay no attention to insider trading
unless, of course, you actually
know somebody.
As volatility can be unpredictable
on foreign exchanges,
past performance truly
cannot ensure future returns,
so try not to invest too heavily
in one sector. And if any advice
you're offered about poetry
simply doesn't sound right,
don't listen.

Michael Colonnese

Back in 2012 I was listening to NPR's Story Corps, *and a victim of the Iraq war, Travis Williams, was telling his story of being the sole survivor of an IED in which eleven others were killed. When I heard this horrible story, I couldn't help but compare it to the daily war news reports that consistently painted the most positive aspects of what was taking place there.*

Contrast

Today we hear our casualties were light.
Good Christ...my leg...the god damned blood, it spurts...
It's been announced the Taliban's in flight.
Please, someone help me...JESUS CHRIST...it hurts.

Good Christ my leg...the god damned blood, it spurts.
Obama says we could bring some boys home.
Please someone, help me, Jesus Christ it hurts.
In Israel they're talking of Shalom.

Obama says we could bring some boys home.
Hey Jack...Where's Jack...I din hear whatcha said.
In Israel they're talking of Shalom.
Hey Jack...oh shit...the motha fucker's dead?

Hey Jack...Where's jack...I din hear whatcha said.
And now, back here at home, we get the word,
Hey Jack...oh shit...the motha fucker's dead.
Munitions firms are healthy, profits soared.

And now, back here at home, we get the word.
It's been announced the Taliban's in flight .
Munitions firms are healthy, profits soared.
Today we hear our casualties were light.

Hal O'Leary

The Liberal Media Made Me Do It

This poem arises from a feature aired sometime in 2012 by Howard Berkes on WVNP, a Wheeling WV NPR station, about the Big Branch coal mine disaster in West Virginia.

Blame

To say there's blame enough to go around,
It means of course that no one will be blamed,
And those responsible will not be found,
With guilty parties never being named.

It means of course that no one will be blamed.
The ethics we once counted on are gone.
With guilty parties never being named,
Gone also is the truth we counted on.

The ethics we once counted on are gone.
Deceit is now the key to one's success.
Gone also is the truth we counted on,
And with it, loss of trust is limitless.

Deceit is now the key to one's success.
It's now "the thing" for one to lie and cheat,
And with it, loss of trust is limitless.
We've got to recognize it as deceit.

It's now the thing for one to lie and cheat,
And those responsible will not be found.
We've got to recognize it as deceit,
To say there's blame enough to go around.

Hal O'Leary

The decision to create a found poem came from re-listening and rereading to see that the lines were there waiting for a poem. The story of the first calls and the meeting with families waiting for any news, the voices of the families of people trapped in the Upper Big Branch Mine, in West Virginia, especially moved me to try and capture their anguish and anger. Using their voices, their words made it more powerful than trying to recap the situation. I listened to the broadcasts on Jefferson Public Radio (JPR) out of Ashland Oregon on 90.9 KSKF, http://ijpr.org/

Into a Void, a Found Poem

Twenty-nine mineworkers died on April 5, 2010, as a fierce explosion ripped through underground entryways. The blast stretched two miles in one direction and three miles in the other, toward the entrance to the mine.
—Upper Big Branch mine, from NPR stories April 2011

And I saw a bright light.
Brightest light I ever saw.
It was what I would describe as hell.
I was truly convinced, truly convinced, that my brother
was going to come out of there alive.

Five sisters waited, day and night
in metal folding chairs on a floor stained with tobacco spit.
Observations did not meet the standards of the protocol.
It was what I would describe as hell.
I saw your loved one. I laid eyes on your loved one.

You have to be absolutely, positively certain;
There were no names associated with bodies.
I saw your loved one. I laid eyes on your loved one.
It was what I would describe as hell.

Five sisters waited, day and night.
All men accounted for. No survivors.
It was absolute, dangerous chaos.
Five sisters waited, on a floor stained with tobacco spit.

And I saw a bright light.
Brightest light I ever saw.
It was what I would describe as hell
I saw your loved one. I laid eyes on your loved one.
I know your loved one is gone.

M.E. Hope

This poem was inspired by a segment of Picture Show, *NPR, April 13, 2013, about the power of the visual image in the occupied West Bank.* Picture Show *led me directly to* Our Harsh Logic: Israeli Soldiers' Testimonies from the Occupied Territories, 2000-2010, *compiled by the organization Breaking the Silence. The radio show and the book made me want to see the extraordinary documentary* Five Broken Cameras *by Emad Burnat and Guy Davidi. The details in the poem—with the exception of the "admired rambunctious uncle," who is fictional, though the mentioned treatment of protestors like him is not—are all drawn from visual images in the film or specifics mentioned in the other two sources.*

What Happens

What happens to the soul of a soldier

Who is struck in the Kevlar vest
        again and again by the fists of screaming
        Palestinian women?

Who pounds on a village door at 1 A.M.
        and rousts the family, the shivering boys
        blinking in the flipped-on light,
        then snaps their pictures, "maps"
        their house, and is gone?

What happens to the photos and the maps
        stuck somewhere in a drawer or "lost"?

What happens to the soul of a soldier
        who shits on a family's sofa
        in their destroyed home?

Does he sleep?

The village children want to sleep, only
        to sleep.

The Liberal Media Made Me Do It

What happens to the soul of a soldier

Who looks on as olive trees are set ablaze
        by settlers?

Who kills a man in an alley at Ramadan
        a man carrying only
        what turns out to be a drum
        to awaken people for breakfast
        before the fast at dawn?

What happens to the soul of a village child
        who watches his family's last olive trees burn?
        who is blasted awake by a stun grenade at 3 A.M.?
        who sees his admired rambunctious uncle dragged off—
        held by each of his four limbs like an animal on the way
        to market—or watches him beaten,
        or martyred?

        What will be his joy?

        The soldier is "mapping" politely at 1 A.M.
        A boy now sleeps in jeans in case a soldier comes
        Another doesn't want to sleep at all
        He's not aware of maps destroyed, says the Colonel
        He's not aware of arrests that are pointless, says the Colonel
        The soldiers come to a door again

        The olives are bulldozed down
        —Screams, hands in air, arrests, releases—
        The olives are planted
        The olives are bulldozed down
        —Screams, hands in air, arrests, releases—

        But someone's camera points and shoots

Judy Kronenfeld

I wrote the poem after hearing my cousin's interview on Day to Day, *5/28/07. His son, Clark Schwedler had recently died in Iraq and his dad spoke about him on NPR.*

High-water Mark
for Clark Schwedler

Here in silence are 10 more, 12 more.
Boys so soft they only shave for dates;
grampas ready for the shade of retirement.
Mississippi age18 U.S Army, Pennsylvania
age 40 Marines, San Diego 23, my kid's age.
I heard the tail end of my cousin's interview on NPR,
telling how his son, a Navy Seal, got on the *honor roll.*

Hegemony, avarice, immodesty, distinction,
Forsaking illustrative nouns we wear like
a strand of iridescent opals; juveniles
collecting gems, meant to stay hidden in the rock.
Oh, that we would be made obliging,
that we could speak slowly again,
take a constitutional evenings,
that burgeoning children might come back.

Deda Kavanagh

This poem was inspired by footage from Sept. 11 in a documentary aired on KCET (PBS) on 9-11, 2002. When a firefighter is immobile for a certain length of time, an alarm that is sewn into his coat is activated. This alarm sounds like a high pitched warbling. On September 11, 01 the air around the WTC collapse was filled for a time with this sound as hundreds of firefighters were buried under debris.

Something About Crickets

After the world got
Suddenly old and
Manhattan pulled this
Gray blanket tightly
To its neck
The air filled with
An odd sound: A
Warbling of sorts as if
A fleet of tiny alarms
Had gone off simultaneously.

Don't these crickets know that
It's not yet nightfall?
Why can't they just get
Up and dust themselves off
And fly home to their
Families?

RD Armstrong

The Liberal Media Made Me Do It

The source of this poem was an article published on the NPR blog and a spate of others on the debate sparked by the death of Trayvon Martin, and then it led me to other news articles on other teens.

Boy

Flickering in the light of the neighbor's
surveillance camera, you see this boy
pulling the trash bin away from the curb. He is
thirteen, it is ten in the morning, he is a boy
at home with his mother and brother in a blue
house with a porch and a screen door. This boy
doesn't say anything I can hear, because I am looking
at the last moments of his life on tape: this boy,
from this distance— from beyond frame after frame and from
beyond his life because now he is dead. Around this boy,
what was the quality of the light that morning? Was it
warm or musky like the silk of corn, was it milky? This boy,
and this other boy who walked to the corner convenience store
for a can of soda and a bag of sweets: under his hood, this boy—
And the boy that, surely, once in his life, the white
man brandishing the gun must have been? Only a boy,
each of them. Black face, sepia-tinted body stepping from
shadow into warm light: how does he become less than a boy?
On camera, two frantic dogs run circles around the man
and the boy; you might hear the voice of the boy
who pleads for his life. Play it again, and still it is the same:
see the man lunge forward, raise his arm, take aim at the boy.

Luisa A. Igloria
07 19 2013
—*Originally published on* Via Negativa, *poet and publisher Dave Bonta's blog in response to his post "Small Stone (244)".*

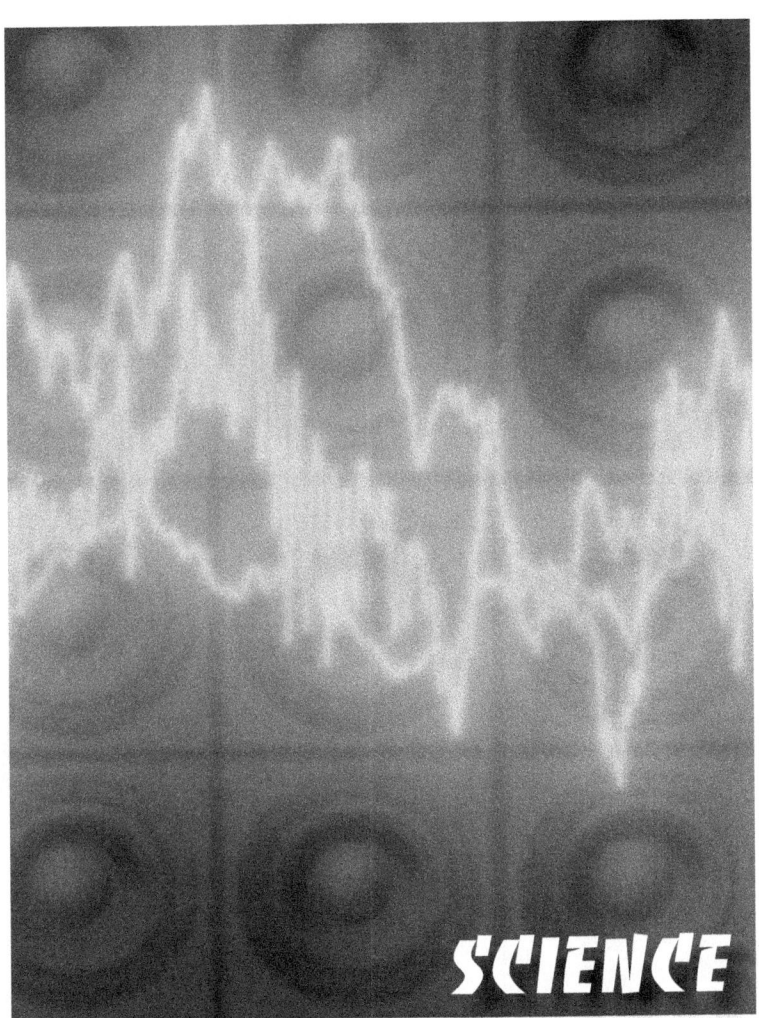

"Cold Front" evolved as I drove to Key West in January of 2010 for the Key West literary seminar, during one of the strongest cold fronts I have ever experienced since moving to the area in 1975. It snowed in 1977 for a few minutes! After that there was one other really cold winter, but I don't remember the date, and then there was 2010. I was driving even further south when I heard on the radio that it was so cold for so long (3-5 days!) that iguanas were going catatonic and dropping out of their trees, fracturing bones, even dying on the sidewalks! As I drove home from Key West, after my conference, I noticed vultures, rather than pelicans, perched all along 7 mile bridge. I later heard on the radio that the fish kill due to the cold weather (temperatures in the Keys were even in the low 30s!) was at a record high. I figured out that's why the vultures were there. It was a startling and unusual sight.

Cold Front in Miami

It didn't snow like back in '77
But it rained iguanas,
Dropping like icicles from trees,
their catatonic bodies too cold to grip,
falling from mango, ficus, cabbage palm,
the hibiscus turned inward and brown,
bromeliads dried up on the spot, wind
sucked them dry, even the fish turned belly up
and vultures circled the bridges, perching
with the pelicans, who warily moved over.
The longest cold front in memory,
a world gone crazy with Floridians
bundled in scarves, coats, mittens,
extra blankets piled on the bed, reading
of earthquakes, landslides, blizzards.
Everyone still waiting for a sign.

Barbra Nightingale
—*Previously published in* Southern Women Writers.
July, 2010.

The Liberal Media Made Me Do It

This poem was inspired by listening to Science Friday *on NPR. I listen to WLRN Miami (91.3) and am both an NPR Junkie and a monthly supporter (albeit in a small way).*

The Weight of It All

Consider the laws of attraction,
how bound we are—or not.
Caught, convoluted, rotating
in a swirl of galaxies.
It's not a question of gravity,

though the situation certainly is grave.
More to the point is matter
how light, how dense,
how dark.
      Light, however, travels straight at an absolute
fixed speed, yet seems to bend
the further it gets.
But it's not the light—it's space
      that corners us, hems us in
or expands to prairies full of lonely.
Perception is a zoom lens—
the closer we are, the larger we appear.
      Everything more immediate
like death
When it's ours, and distant
when it's yours.

Barbra Nightingale

The Liberal Media Made Me Do It

Astronomers infer that some matter, invisible to current modes of detection, exists in the more than 80 percent of space once believed empty. Its presence is linked to ideas about the continuing expansion of the universe. Italicized lines in the poem are quoted from the February 25, 2000 airing of the National Public Radio show "Talk of the Nation: Science Friday" *that I heard on KQED San Francisco.*

Dark Matter

In 1929, Edwin Hubble theorized that the universe was expanding.
In 1998, scientists found evidence that this expansion was speeding up.

It is only the space between stars.

Only matter, falling away from itself:

the dark and missing
side of the universe—

earth, air, fire, water,
quintessence the fifth element

—everything now is farther but gets there
faster: light in the wires, your hand
as it lifts toward your face, more distant

by an atom than the day before. A spilled drink
moves across the table at six feet
per second, but so too does the cloth.

We have direct evidence from the supernovae.

In the backyard, over the wading pool,
the clothesline: crack and warble

of the satellites, their tethers webbed and straining
above our heads.

Lisa Gluskin Stonestreet

This is a found poem created by combining words and phrases from the following NPR reports: "Antibiotic-Resistant Bugs Turn Up Again in Turkey Meat"; "Antibiotic Use on the Farm: Are We Flying Blind?"; "Are Farm Veterinarians Pushing Too Many Antibiotics?"; "Bacterial Competition in Lab Shows Evolution Never Stops"; "Bird, Plane, Bacteria? Microbes Thrive in Storm Clouds"; "Booming Demand for Donated Breast Milk Raises Safety Issues"; "Could Detectives Use Microbes to Solve Murders?"; "Getting Your Microbes Analyzed Raises Big Privacy Issues" and "Thriving Gut Bacteria Linked to Good Health."

All Bacteria Considered

Eat and divide. Eat and divide. They are alive
you know, in an active state. They are alive

down the noses of 6-month-old cattle,
on our skin, on a corpse, in breast milk

sold on the Internet. They are alive
thriving in gut microbiomes

in yogurts, in turkeys raised conventionally.
Bad guys, like E. coli, Salmonella

Heidelberg, eat and divide
sort of fly blind, end up

in people in various ways.
The bacteria on a person who died

naturally may look different
than the bacteria on someone

who was beaten to death.
We want the good kind

The Liberal Media Made Me Do It

the anti-inflammatory, the beneficial
actinobacteria. The Q-tip quickly turns

a greasy brown: sharing body fluids
is fecal bacteria Russian roulette.

Not exactly a friendly place
but the bacteria seem able to handle it.

Kelly Nelson

I heard the story that inspired this poem, "Holey Cow," on Radiolab, *which I listen to on radio station KPCC.*

Fistulated Cow

After a Story on Radiolab

Beneath a shield of hide and flesh
the cow's stomach hangs
like a hammock from the triangular
scaffolding of the pelvis.
You've always guessed it was there
that alchemical apparatus
working away in the steamy darkness,
transmuting grass and hay
to silky curds, an ivory flow.
But now, you can see for yourself.
No need to hang back, to cower there
in a corner. Slip on those rubber gloves.
Enter the inner chamber.

We think of the stomach as a sack,
soft and loose as a pocket
in a much-laundered jacket.
It's more like a muscle.
Feel it grab your hand,
sucking the fingers down
into the vortex where intestines,
ribbed as a vacuum cleaner hose,

The Liberal Media Made Me Do It

coil, and the sweet grass
travels the length of each helix,
each pearly arc, like tourists
queued at Disneyland, and the billions
of bugs do their work. And in you as well
the same mysterious everyday magic
you don't like to think about
goes on.
        Now we'll put back the plug,
let the cow wade knee-high into a field of clover,
a body linked to other bodies,
making the most of the world.

Robbi Nester

First published in 3Elements Review
    Denise Herzing is a marine biologist who studies wild dolphins in Bermuda. I heard about her research on interspecies communication on All Things Considered.

Exchange

For Denise Herzing and the Wild Dolphin Project

The shoreline shimmers in the distance
barely half there, the only real thing
this shifting sea, blue line of sky.
We are here to speak with the dolphins.
For six years we have followed them,
scanning the depths off Bermuda, clear as air.
We know each one by its behavior,
its singular expression. They permit us
to study them, and clearly
study us as well, have learned
to tell us from each other.
I proffer a fish to an eager male.
The dolphin's comical mouth
with its permanent grin and conical
teeth so different from our own,
opens to receive an offering of herring
on a tongue the color and the shape
of a child's pink plastic shovel
as an enormous yellow keyboard,
keys the size of street signs, drops
in slow motion from the ship.
The diver slips into the water,
his black suit shining like the dolphins'
own slick skin. Again and again,
with one gloved hand, the diver
strikes a key etched with the bright
likeness of a beach ball, and each time

The Liberal Media Made Me Do It

a shower of balls falls all around.
The curious dolphins gather, leaping
from the flat grey sea. Most merely watch,
but at last, one approaches,
punches the button with her blunt snout,
and the balls splash to the surface.
At this moment, there is language,
an exchange and an understanding.
It is not as we imagined, this first contact,
in the ocean that is, yet is not, our home.
We have dreamed of space, its empty
airless miles, an uncharted sea of stars
where we might meet our alien other,
hearing and being heard by the light
of other suns. Instead, we encounter
these familiar strangers
their rubbery faces like masks,
in this, our common ground
of sea under the ordinary moon.
We are awkward and polite as pilgrims
meeting the native tribes,
neighbors on the earth we share.

Robbi Nester

The Liberal Media Made Me Do It

In July 2010, Talk of the Nation *host Ira Flato invited Digital Media Editor Flora Lichtman into the studio to discuss Video Pick of the Week. Lichtman describes the footage as X-rated, joking about the mating habits of horseshoe crabs—as one might expect of a species that performs coitus in orgies along the eastern coast, from Maine to the Yucatan, during the summer. Lighthearted banter aside, I rejoiced in the fact that Lichtman communicated how much humans owe to the ancient marine creatures, the important role they play for migrating birds, and why we should cherish these "living fossils." Come Memorial Day, for the past four years, our family has made the trip to Delaware to see the horseshoe crabs at play. Some may find these spiders of the sea (as I think of them) bizarre looking, if not repulsive. I feel only affection for them, and hope that, having survived this long, environmentalists will do whatever possible to assure their continued survival.*

Limulus Polyphemus

300 million years is quite a record.
If anything can survive mass extinction
it might be the colloquial horse-
shoe crab, as if by any other name
the little beast would repulse the tourists,
the gardeners that spread what remains
of their barnacled shells once ground
into fertilizer, the patients in need
of the next miracle drug.

A living fossil is rare enough,
even if you believe your husband mal-
adaptive or your children an alien
species. Even if her mother called her
boyfriend a freak or his best friend
is a komodo dragon, tongue flicking,
lidded eyes and bad breath. Or
you woke with that primordial angst
you get after a fitful night's sleep.

The Liberal Media Made Me Do It

Shaped like a shovel, armored
and encamped on the warm sands
of Dewey Beach, the blue blooded
Limulus is time's own riddle, ancient—
yet in so many ways a novelty.

Kathryn Kopple

It's almost irresistible to describe animals in human terms. It's certainly easier for humans to understand animals if we give them human motives and reactions. Even though it was several years ago, I vividly remember watching this documentary about the white-eared cob. The narration was so annoying that I started jotting down bits of it. Later, I used those bits in "Mute."

I can't find that particular documentary. Since then, I've become conscious of how animals are described in these programs. I've noticed that, on PBS, scientists and photographers who often are the narrators are more likely to stick to description. I appreciate that. However, a quick look at a few Nature episodes turned up monkeys with "punk hairstyles" and eagles described as a "couple." As I said, it's irresistible. And sometimes, I just want to punch the mute button.

Mute

I'm not quibbling over the photography
in those nature documentaries. It's stunning,
and I marvel at how the camera captures

the moment. The bloody, frothing water as the crocodile
strikes. The wave breaking around a walrus.
It's the narration that's so annoying: *The young*

emerge from the battlefield older and wiser. Really?
It's the Disneyfication of the critters that gets me,
the rampant anthropomorphism, the cutesiness.

*Hardly anyone knows the neighborhood leopard
is there.* Really? Done a poll? Asked the *neighbors*?
Often the narration is unnecessary: *The powerful sharp*

hooves descend on the reptiles again and again. I'm
watching the again and again, for Pete's sake. And always
the pregnant pause. The plummy tone. The over-

The Liberal Media Made Me Do It

careful enunciation, dulcet, mellifluous, smarmy.
The mournful strings of the full orchestra crescendo.
I imagine the long faces as they saw away underscoring

the death of the white-eared cob in the jaws of the croc . . .
fading, fading, vibrating, silently beating. . . leaving only
the echoes of the chorus's wordless incantation as the water

stills. The narrator, insistent on having the last word,
wringing every last bit of pathos, says, one grandiose,
terminal, truism: *Death is as vital ... as life.*

Anne Baber

"Eating in Winter" was inspired by an episode of Engines of Our Ingenuity, *which is produced by the Houston NPR affiliate.*

Eating in Winter

Whatever meat
clings to
the ring

of rib cage
chanced upon
in beak-deep

snow beckons,
but a raven
will not eat

alone, the whole
constable bowing
among bones

defies Darwin's
survival-of
as their nibs

clink against each other
like gold links.
Instead of

exchanging jewelry,
let's peel
the clementines.

I'll let you
eat all
the sections.

Barbara Duffey

This poem is based on an episode of Radiolab *(WNYC – New York) entitled* Space, *which I heard as a podcast. This* Radiolab *episode was one of the first I had ever heard, and featured Carl Sagan's widow, Ann Druyan, sharing the story of their professional relationship and eventual romance, in the context of their work on the Voyager spacecraft. The idea of "space" in terms of human relationships set this poem in motion.*

Radiolab: Space

Huddle with me over astral maps, let's climb this ladder
to the stars, to Alberio, naked-eye bright, so we can open
our palms, stretch our fingers, and seem to touch it.

If only the pulse and pull of my blood
could reach through the dark matter.

You say where we are is a matter of perspective,
a perspective of matter, our story
etched on a gold record, voyaging
billions of years from now, a story
delicate as a deer's ear, flawed as first words.

Here on earth, flowing streams leave messages for us
on their banks – a bluejay feather, an arrowhead,
a bear's pawprint.

A recipe of "us" includes ash, glass,
and concrete grammar of Bach, floating
from our bodies like notes from a flute.
Stars mark directions, but don't control
the currents of bodies, streams, or oceans.

The Liberal Media Made Me Do It

Each word we utter expands to make
its own space, filling a never place —
the silence after the big bang, drowning out
the voices of the other curling dimensions.

So come, meet your shoulder to mine
as we chart these stars together, trace
the outlines of birds, heroes, and bears;
the story, our story, hasn't ended.
There is no edge to the universe.

Kris Bigalk

This story comes from PBS' science hotline 08/28/2013

USDA Drops Poison On Guam

For seventy years, adventure seeking Australian Brown Snakes have hitched rides on cargo ships bound for Guam. Once there, the snakes discovered they had no natural predators. They've thrived, multiplied, gobbled up the native birds, started in on small animals. They fall from trees onto the heads and roofs of unsuspecting humans. They become tangled in electric lines and short out whole areas of the island. In hopes of controlling the snakes, the Department of Agriculture has dropped little paper parachutes carrying poison-laced frozen mice.

Photographs show hundreds of white mice floating toward the forest. Imagine a snake's surprise at hearing helicopters overhead, seeing dinner wafting like manna from the sky, never suspecting that this bounty, this good fortune, this mouse brings with it just one baby Tylenol, enough to destroy the liver of a snake.

Patricia L. Scruggs

The Liberal Media Made Me Do It

This poem was inspired by a Radiolab *story aired on KPCC FM November 10, 2013. The story was included on an episode of the show called "Emergence." It was about ants and highlighted how their trial-and-error investigations of the world mimic what we think of as intelligence.*

Leaf-Cutter Ants

You should see us
      go after a paperback
  especially once
          rain
has made jam
      of the binding.
A true commie plot
      we will chew your state
department
  from inside
      bury it
dig it up and bury it
      and dig it up and . . .
You get the picture. Mastication
      are us—we can even use
  the subjunctive.
We will feed your culture,
your self-portrait,
    to you
as if you were our child—relentlessly.
      No pity. No pride.
      No picnics.

Richard Nester

This poem was based on a Science Friday *story on Oct. 18 on KXJZ in Sacramento where I listened to it.*

The Trees and the Vines

Snaking up the trees are the vines.
The old rivals return to their incriminations,
their calls to order the forest.
The vines love the edges and swarm
the openings; they use the small trees
as trellises and camp in the sky.
The canopy is reconfigured.
It is reassembled with the new brand
of rodent intact, the invader
that will eat anything.
Its opportunity is the next
chapter in the mythic battle of
tree and vine. All these years
the two have been locked into
a balance that is now upset.
The tree as giver is standing
still for the hungry vine
to dominate, to reject its kindness
as carbon sink and oxygen
bringer. The trees bring care
and quiet into the system,
enough to make us wonder —
will the charitable survive
in numbers sufficient
to replenish their kind?

Tim Kahl

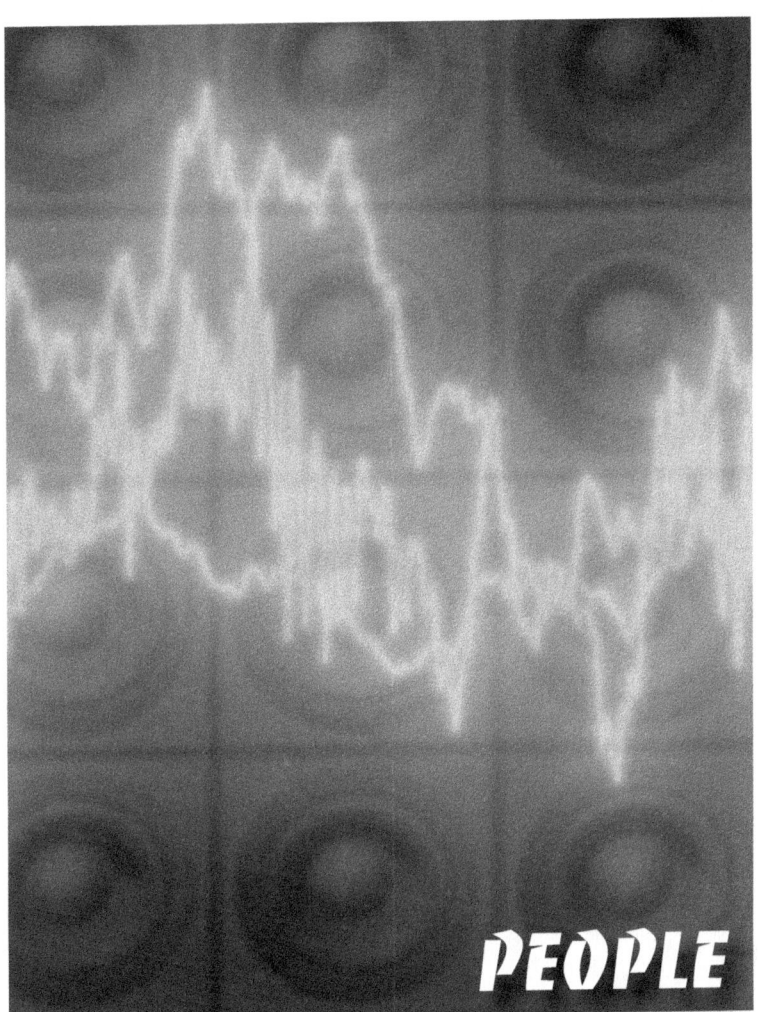

"Scientist" is based on the segment "From Benford to Erdos" from the podcast Numbers, *which originally aired on November 30, 2009. I was taken with the story of the life of the Hungarian mathematician Paul Erdos, a man who took so much joy in doing mathematics, and was so good at it, that he would crash at mathematician friends' houses and wake them up at four in the morning to do math problems. His passion and talent, as described on* Radiolab, *inspired me to write this poem.*

Radiolab: Scientist

Shoes, heavy brown leather with buckskin laces, confine the feet,
limit the expansion of ideas in the blood, constrict toes and thoughts,
rub against heel and bunion, reminding him of mortality. This monk
of science had no use for shoelaces, clocks, mealtimes. The body,
such a transient bundle of cells, but the mind burns like a star
gathering itself to a blue-hot focus, a flash before the supernova
that tears open a hole in the fabric of yesterday, of the body's slow
decline, sped up. Letters stained with the tea or coffee of the day,
but otherwise void of everyday objects, food, conversation. He
had no home for the body, the mind needed none, anchoring itself
to the constellations, a pen, pencil, paper, sky.

Kris Bigalk

"Seeing" is based on a Radiolab Short called "Seeing in the Dark," which I heard on KNOW in Minneapolis on October 22, 2012. One of the things I love about the Radiolab show is that they often compare and contrast opinions and experiences of two different people. This episode explored the experience of blindness from the perspectives of two different men, and how each processed information and imagined their lives differently. The idea of what we really "see" versus what we imagine sparked this poem.

Seeing

The cataract grayed, then blackened to blindness.
Now I feel the boredom of the fortunate
who have nothing to observe, to consider.
My wife has no reason to buy a new red dress or smash feet
into spike heels, straighten or color her silken hair,
massage expensive creams into her neck and face each night.
She exists only in a photograph I remember on a shelf in a corner of my mind.

I stop picturing. My mind turns as black as the backs of my retinas.
When I walk down a corridor, or stand at a window, I am cold.
The vibrations of the glass make different music than the muffled walls.

I choose not to see the truth with details missing.
I imagine nothing, instead of everything.
The truth is blank, a white screen with a soundtrack.
My child is a giggle, a tap of tiny feet on my chest, a warm cheek
I lay my hand upon, to feel his soft breathing when he sleeps.

Kris Bigalk

I was fascinated by the NPR/PBS stories of Mike May, a man who had lost his sight as a young child, but had recovered most of it in his forties. I was mostly struck by his comment about his wife—that he could recognize her more easily with his eyes closed. I thought of the blind man in the Bible and this poem (a pantoum) is the result.

The Forest of Her

I see people, but they look like trees walking
    ~the healed blind man to Jesus, book of Mark
I crave an intimacy too private to speak of,
    truly one must close one's eyes to see.
        ~Marvin Bell

Perhaps, after all, we should embrace our darkness
for that Bible story may have had things wrong.
Like knowledge, a little sight can be dangerous,
for he once was blind, but even now he can't see.

That Bible story may have had things wrong:
the poor man cannot now recognize his own wife.
He once was blind, but even now he can't see
the length of her hair and her particular gait.

That poor man cannot now recognize his own wife
by sight. He knows her only by her scent,
the length of her hair, and her particular gait:
the faithful whisper of air moving

slightly, lifting from her to him her scent
as if a secret spoken in darkness.
The faithful whisper of air moving
reveals her in the half-light of half-sight.

The Liberal Media Made Me Do It

As if a secret spoken in darkness,
her body grows mysterious roots.
Revealed, in the half-light of half-sight,
the leaves of hair, her branching arms—

her body grown mysterious. Roots
and limbs tangle, quaking the shadowy
leaves of hair. Her branching arms
catch him like a weary bird at day's end.

His limbs tangle, quaking in the shadowy
places of her body. The familiar forest of her
catches him like a weary bird. At day's end
he closes his eyes and finds his way

around her body—the familiar forest of her
like knowledge. A little sight can be dangerous,
so he closes his eyes and finds his way
for perhaps, after all, we should embrace our darkness.

Christina Lovin
  —Previously published in Levure Litteraire *(a French journal)*

"Comatose" is based on a segment called "Finding Emilie" from the Radiolab *podcast episode called* Lost and Found, *which originally aired on January 25, 2011.* Radiolab *is a production of WNYC in New York. One line from this podcast stuck with me for days, and eventually I wrote it down and the poem began: "Pull me out of this wall." The story, of a woman who regains consciousness after a terrible head injury, was so moving, as was the dedication of her significant other, that the poem seemed to write itself in a more effortless way than many of my other poems.*

Comatose

Pull me out of this wall,
spell me with letters traced on my back,
my thigh, my wrist, traced with fingertips
light as a daisy petal. Pull me out
of this plaster, this stasis, sing me out with rhymes
against the cartilage of my ears, loud as trumpets.
Pull me past the studs, the framing, conjugate
the verbs of my muscles, bend my arms until
they fold around your shoulders. Pull me from
behind the pipes and outlets, coax the words
from my throat as you would a butterfly
from its chrysalis, with slow, light presses
of the thumb, until the edge cracks, and
my first words emerge with wet wings,
fervent, trembling.

Kris Bigalk

—*"Comatose" appears in the poetry collection* Repeat the Flesh in Numbers *(New York Quarterly Books, 2012), and in* Poetry City, USA, Volume 2 *(LowBrow Press, 2012).*

The Liberal Media Made Me Do It

"Living Will" is based on a Radiolab *episode called* The Bitter End. *In this episode, one of the hosts, Jad Abumrad, interviews his father, a medical doctor, about his last wishes in terms of being revived. That conversation, along with other sobering facts about end of life realities presented in the podcast, led me to write this persona poem.*

Living Will (*Radiolab*: The Bitter End)

Don't
beat me
back from death
don't feed me let
me waste let
morphine snow down
so warm behind
my eyes. The tel-
evision fiction happy
endings in ER's
lives saved pain
erased I will not
be wakened
by a kiss rib-cracking
chest compressions
starting up my
heart don't breathe
for me, I will fight
intubations,
motionless, every
cell mouthing
a tiny
scream

Tattoo "No Code"
on my wrist,
my chest

Comfort me soften
the pillow under
my head, hold me
against your regular
beats, no beep
of machine

The last day we
spent together
like this I had
just loosened you
from my body,
and I held
you until
you slept.

Kris Bigalk
— *"Living Will" was originally published under a different title in* Revolver.

Here is a poem based on a Frontline *story I saw years ago about an Earthquake survivor in China.*

Like the Wings of the Butterfly

The miner, Wang Shu Bin,
tells the story of his last
hours with his wife:
trapped within the rubble
of his hospital ward
after a devastating earthquake
"My wife called to me
in the darkness, we were both pinned
under debris, "Wang Shu Bin! Are you
alive?' I said "yes, can you move?"
She said, "I am pinned from the waist
down." I began to claw away at the
cement blocks that buried me. It took
two days for me to reach her. She
was only three beds away
from me. I tried to get to her but a large
beam blocked her from me. I could only
touch her fingers. When she realized I was
beside her, she was so glad, her fingers
fluttered like the wings of a butterfly.
For two more days we talked of our past,
of our love for each other. Throughout
her fingers touched mine, speaking to my
heart, directly. Finally, she said one word to me.
"Wang," and the butterfly ceased to flutter.

RD Armstrong

The sinking of the Kursk and subsequent death of the crew (and the poignant letter discovered later) was covered several times on both PBS and NPR: PBS News Hour, *another PBS program* Secrets of the Kursk *(date unknown),* BBC News, *and so on.*

Writing Blindly

I am writing blindly.
—Dimitri Kolexnikov, of the doomed Russian
 submarine, Kursk, in a letter to his wife

This is my dying
message. I am dying.
My message may live. I would
write in blood without
an instrument, with my finger-
nails, with intense pain on the stone
wall of my prison, the rusted
door of this crypt, inside
the coffin lid—scratches, clawings.
Symbols that are untranslatable
to calm eyes, unutterable
to steady voices.

I want to tell you to sing
because a song is sweeter
in the dark, to tell you the dark
is sweeter than light, that light
is sweeter than death, that death
is light when inhalation becomes
the rumor of a dead man's
smile, and pulse
is a lie of rhythm;
when all that can be
written is the myth,
the flourish
turning my last breath
to vapor.

The Liberal Media Made Me Do It

I am writing blindly
in the language of the living
who are already dead.

I am writing blindly.

Like all of us.

Christina Lovin
—*Previously published in* Best Poem.

The Liberal Media Made Me Do It

There have been a number of NPR/PBS shows regarding race in the past few years, it's hard to put my finger on one in particular. However, I believe the "Freedom Riders" episode was one of the most memorable. The white woman who, at twelve, offered water to those who had nearly escaped death in the bus fire moved me greatly, as I would have been that same age when the incident happened. I grew up in a mixed neighborhood (although we were the last house on the street with a white family), and did not understand what was happening around me.

A Cup of White Sugar

In the fifties, in my town, on my street,
segregation was a word
we didn't know. At least in my house. Not me:
my mother would send me to the neighbor's
for a loaf of bread, some lard, a cup of white
flour or sugar, weekly if not more. Mrs. Gatlin

(Florence I would come to know later)
was gentle and kind, offering me
on every visit a piece of ribbon candy:
stripes of color—red, yellow, green—against white
satiny sweetness, stretched, then swirled
back onto themselves over and over again.

Her house, like her, was neat and dark
and smelled of pork hocks and greens,
cornbread in iron skillets. Her daughter
a princess in pink chiffon and white
lace-trimmed anklets with shiny black
Mary Janes. Her sons like shadow-

twins to my brothers. We children of the same
block of unpaved streets and ditches
filled with weeds and empty liquor
bottles played side by side until
one dark boy and I joined in a game
of Cowboys and Indians. Mrs. Gatlin saw us –

The Liberal Media Made Me Do It

him patting me down to check for six-shooters
or knives, as I lay prone in the grass, felled
by an imaginary bullet: a scenario played out
every Saturday of our young lives
on the TV westerns all we children watched,
where white gunmen shot the bad guys,

Mexicans outlaws, or the ubiquitous
Indians. She must have told my mother.
Duane and I never played together again.
I couldn't understand. All the while
I rode my old, blind horse past thin-walled
shanties at the end of the street far from ours

(the only white house on Pennsylvania),
Soon enough I would stand again, impatient,
oblivious child, in that clean, dim living room
while Mrs. Gatlin fetched a cup of white
sugar from her fragrant kitchen and placed
in my pale, open hand that bright, twisted candy.

Christina Lovin
—*Previously published in* Cold Shoulders, Evil Eyes
(Wising Up Press) and in Flesh *(Finishing Line Press)*

This piece was inspired by a story on Marketplace *(NPR):*
http://www.npr.org/blogs/money/2013/12/03/247360855/two-sisters-a-small-room-and-the-world-behind-a-t-shirt

Textile

"dusty fields. A white sun above. All this road, going." ~ Dorothea Lange

The line is a thread. The thread is a piece in a weft of fabric. The thread pushed forward and back by the bobbin, from a pin, from an implement that pushes the furrows and turns the field into rows and rows. Today I listened to the radio story on two sisters, factory pieceworkers in Bangladesh. How the older one was married off to a man chosen by her parents because they thought he would be able to provide. The reporter said she didn't laugh anymore. She is maybe 23, has a daughter, 7 years old, cared for by others in the village. But she talks about not wanting to visit the family home because she is angry at her parents who have ruined her life. The reporter says *I am sorry, I made you cry*. The younger sister did not have to do the same thing— by the time she hit her teens, there was one other choice besides arranged marriage: go to work in the factory. I see in my mind's eye hundreds of girls like her, thousands, washing in the commons behind the building, twisting their damp hair into knots. Think of shadows in the alleys interrupted by the fluttering flags of laundry hanging from tenement windows. The soot on the walls from their kerosene lamps, the meal they will share, sitting on their haunches on the floor. A curtain doubles as a door, doubles as a wall, a screen. But there is a TV. And a cellphone. They talk about how they make T-shirts: what stitches, what seams, how the collar must come to a point at the bottom of the V. Endless days like these. Like a road they hope will take them somewhere better. Every now and then a torn fingernail, close brush with the needle and the cutter. One of the girls thinks with a start of the thousand bodies folded and crushed, thin as cloth beneath stone. She was only thinking of the rhinestone earrings she bought at the market stall, of wearing them on the next free day, an outing at the coast.

Luisa A. Igloria 12-3-2013
—*Previously published on* Via Negativa, *poet and publisher Dave Bonta's blog, where Igloria has posted responses to comments in the form of poetry for over two years. She has posted a poem daily for over three years.*

The Liberal Media Made Me Do It

The subject matter of this poem is sexual abuse and repressed memory. I have heard several programs on this topic on NPR. The most recent was Neal Conan's on Talk of the Nation, *June 19, 2012. It was entitled "What is Behind the Silence of Sexual Abuse?"*

I listen to three NPR Stations, but WSDL (90.7) is my home station.

pulled blinds

hint
       of Aqua Velva
in Safeway/ in Starbucks/ in any crowd
       triggers
pain   violent as poison

roller-coaster spasms
this morning's ham and eggs

another shrink
       probes
fragmented secrets   shadow memories
       bolted doors of childhood

a man's hard hand
across my mouth
hint of Aqua Velva
       the earth quakes beneath me

afterwards a banana split

Kit Zak

SWS-87: The Voice of Rachel

*A voice is heard in Ramah lamenting and weeping bitterly;
it is Rachel weeping for her children, refusing to be
comforted for her children, because they are no more."
Jeremiah 31:15; Matthew 2:18*

I am SWS-87
eleven birthday candles blown
in a place I didn't know was heaven
a place I just called home, Ledici;
Ledici, Bosnia! It sang my tongue!
Four birthdays   no candles blown
in a place I now call hell.

It was April 1992   they came
spring rain resting like wool
on the mountain. They
took me to a filthy cell
for "interrogation purposes".
Accused of lying
my girl body quivered
like a sapling tree.
They stripped me bare
and climbed me there
five   rough   men
a pimpled boy
always one   laughing
watching   pressing his gun
to my head   my god the smell
of them   their swollen members
blades between my legs.
They numbered me   SWS-87
and I survived to tell.

The Liberal Media Made Me Do It

They took me to my school
where I had learned my numbers
how to read and write and play
and say my name   and locked me
with the others; girls   cousins
lamenting mothers   Auntie B.
We were ashamed. At first
we hardly spoke   the bitter weeping
of our dreams provoked the drunken
guard. We soon became their raping pool
they used us every day. For me
it happened in the night   they took
me to the gymnasium   had their fill
when games were done. And hell
went on   and on   and on
eight months or more.
But I had learned my numbers
how to read and write and play
and say my name. I am SWS-87
and I survived to tell.

One night they set me naked
on a table like a jug of wine
commanded me to dance
for Montenegrin officers.
One purchased me for
two week's pay and took me
to his private hole to have his way.

The Liberal Media Made Me Do It

When terror finally bled
into the chambers of the law
our woman stories were
"too embarrassing to consider
in court." For *our woman shame
our guilt* many   even sisters
want to silence us. "There are things
outsiders should never know," they say.*
I tremble speaking out. My daily fear
reprisals   on my friends
and family   the ones
who have not disappeared.
But I am now fifteen. I have
learned my numbers
how to read and write and play
and say my name. I am SWS-87
I am not ashamed.

Martha O. Adams
—Previously published in my collection, What Your Heart
  Needs to Know *(House of Myrrth; 2008)*

The Liberal Media Made Me Do It

There was an article on NPR that got me really thinking about anorexia - the fact that we'd have to resort to such a radical treatment. I got to thinking about how women start to descend into it. Most start as adolescents, but several women start to resort to it when their body image gets thrown too far out of whack.

Thinning

Her morning meal, no more
smoothies of grapefruit,
protein powder, kelp—
she gagged on the flavor,
the feel in her mouth,
but choked more
on herself, squishy
thighs, belly spilling over
ever tighter jeans
already two sizes up.
Her breasts puffed
as well, but the cleavage
felt almost obscene, not
sexy but a sign
her body wanted
to envelop itself.
So her morning starts
with two cups
of coffee, two smokes,
two shots. Muddled
at first, but
her weight drops,
a hot air balloon
settling, a slack
collapse. So two
became three,
woozy and craving
became one. Her smell
changes from an earthy
musk to a sharp

The Liberal Media Made Me Do It

smell of grass just
starting to decay.
She trades in lunch
too, it works, it all
works, brings her back
to bones showing
under skin. She
figures a few months,
enough to feel a new
self, to be
a compost heap,
slow rot to shrink
her down until
she filters all
that is wrong.
She tries hard
to remember slight
breezes against the hair on
her arms, the languish
of a slow pulse. She
no longer thinks
of the taste
of fresh-baked bread
or cantaloupe.

Amy MacLennan

The story that inspired this poem was a BBC program broadcast on NPR entitled Heart and Soul *on Monday June 13th, 2011. The program aired in Richmond, VA: 88.9 WCVE.*

  Here is a description from the show's website of the program's content: "Vietnam is over-run with ghosts. To pass onto the next world, you need to die well - in old age, body unblemished, the proper rituals observed. But few of the five million people killed in the Vietnam War were granted such a peaceful ending. They became "wandering souls" - doomed to eke out an impoverished existence on the edge of the everyday world."

My Brother's Wandering Soul

Over 300,000 bodies of Vietnamese soldiers have still not been found by their families.

I fold buoyant blue paper into a boat
that will deliver my light down

the Hoi An river. Spirit fish
carry my lantern with hundreds more

so the hồn ma can follow
these guides to Nirvana. My brother

visits me, and I witness his death

an explosion leaf-wrapped
on Ho Chi Min trail.

I travel on a red shiny scooter,
to and from my job in the city.

My ears are pierced
three times, my nails are waxen

and long. I use these nails to shred
my chest when my brother visits.

The Liberal Media Made Me Do It

I rip my windy tomb open. The scar

tissue will not heal. Bits of bone
expose themselves through my flesh.

Over this, I wear an expensive red bra
and silk blouse. My body is a moving grave

where we reunite. My brother's soul gnashes

my breastbone, tears me
asunder. His body is lost

in jungle heavy cover.
His arms are strung in the tree limbs.

With my two lives I waltz
a perfect circle, one an eyeless begging tiger,

the other floats down the Hoi An river,
a pledge to the dead more than the living.

Brittney Scott
—*This poem originally appeared in* Prairie Schooner.

The Liberal Media Made Me Do It

All the details in the poem came from a story on All Things Considered. *I don't remember exactly when it aired.*

His Eye

Somewhere where terrible things happen—
not here, though terrible things do happen—
but somewhere they happen more frequently
(and I read about this, I didn't see it first hand),
a boy was beaten so fiercely that one eyeball
fell out of his head, and he carried his own eye
safe in the palm of his hand over many miles
to the nearest doctor and begged the doctor
please to sew his eye back in its raw socket
but of course the doctor couldn't sew it back
(I suppose the optic nerve was severed and
who knows what all else) so that loose eye
was thrown out or buried, who knows which,
because that detail wasn't in the story I heard,
but here's what I do know: forever afterward
the boy's hand, the hand that carried the eye,
was gifted with vision. If he touched a stone,
he knew the hidden inside color of that stone,
and when he grew up and touched a woman,
he knew, more fully than anyone else could,
all the untold dread that made her beautiful.

Penelope Scrambly Schott
—*Previously published in* The New Guard *and forthcoming in* How I Became an Historian, *Schott, 2014.*

The Liberal Media Made Me Do It

Margaret Warner did a wonderful interview on Friday, October 11, 2013 on the News Hour *(PBS) with Malala Yousafazai, the young girl shot by the Taliban in Pakistan for defending a girl's right to receive an education.. My local public television station here in Hallandale Beach, Florida is WPBT, based in Miami but serving the entire South Florida region. It's also the oldest public television station in the state.*

Her Education

Into the quiet classroom
of the mind comes flying
the furious teacher with a lesson
of fear. This *bullet*
is not a bullet, it's merely
a word, something the mouth
makes for the delicate ear,
something the breath sends
that troubles the air, a ballet
of sound moving through silence
that explodes in an image as sudden
as death. Where is the wound?
It bleeds in the minds of a million
grief-stricken girls. They will be
pilots, doctors, warriors,
poets. They will sit on the ground
in the dust, just to learn.
In the twenty-first century,
every girl is Malala.

Meryl Stratford
—*Previously appeared in* Malala: Poems for Malala Yousafzai *(FutureCycle Press, available at Amazon.com)*

From Sonnets for the Lost and Surviving

This sonnet project is meant to be a feminist re-reading of the official 9/11 story, involving a feminized sonnet pattern and message. It is meant to accompany a thoughtful public in moving forward and demanding a reliable and independent investigation of the history and consequences of the events we call "9/11."

Sonnets for the Lost and Surviving

Two fell together, holding hands

I woke dreaming clocks reversed plans
rotating back upside down yet
I'm not late Time for coffee get
a paper then the train expands
to fill and release Here I met
you the first time and here we go
together sometimes and although
my heart shifts for you my mind's set
but then bombs and fire and then no
thing can save us not magic wands
carpets flying Today we met
fire surrendered to holding hands
falling By dying we'll forget
this day but I'll remember you

Kirstin Bratt

Down the stairs

He ordered me upstairs I ran
down instead frightened all amiss
smoke mirrors wide gaping abyss
Never mind orders Peter Pan
just run fly whatever near miss
you can manage for troubled times
as these Sounding vague scattered crimes
unrivaled horror in the hiss
of bombs of glass of nursery rhymes
rock-a-bye the gingerbread man
London bridge falls and death's damp kiss
melts in the morning fire A plan
for night fall for day light All this
for traitors The rough clanging chimes

Kirstin Bratt

From a PBS documentary, Caught In the Crossfire, *2002*

After a Testimony by Usman Farman

I worked in building seven
of the Towers. That day,
I waited for the train
under a sky of sheerest
silk stretched taut, pinned
in the corner by a shadow moon.
When the first plane hit,
I don't remember hearing it,
just seeing smoke, black
billows sullying that perfect sky.

"Go north," they told us,
"and do not look back."
We went five blocks, but
none of us could help
turning to watch the tower fall.
Against that sky, a china
bowl without a crack,
a fifty-story cloud of glass
and dust rose up, pursued us
like a vision born of dream or scripture.

I ran, but soon fell to the ground,
face burning in brown-gray air.
I could not will my legs to move,
but watched the world grow dark.
Then, as though the dust
had taken form,
a man stood at my side.

The Liberal Media Made Me Do It

He wore the black garb
of Hasidic Jews: fur hat,
side locks, and beard.
Stooping to scan the amulet
I wore, a prayer in Arabic,
he looked me in the face,
saying, "Brother, grab my hand."
I cannot say how long we ran—
it seemed forever, and we
never looked behind.
When I stopped, the man
was gone, and I was safe.

I've asked myself
why I live, not the rest.
Anyone can be a messenger.
Survival may rely
on an extended hand.

Robbi Nester

—This poem was previously published in HEArt.

The Liberal Media Made Me Do It

I first heard the ongoing story about the last Jew of Afghanistan on NPR. Why does he stay when his family and congregation left long ago? What does he do? He tries to maintain the last synagogue despite being rundown and abandoned while running a small café. This universal feeling of isolation we all feel at one time, he must experience on a continual basis to some degree. So, if you listen long enough to NPR and BBC and other news stories, you, too, can find inspiration and hear the poetry of our lives being told— all you have to do is go write it.

The Last Days of the Balkh Bastan (2013)

Zablon Simintov is the last Jew of Afghanistan
& owner of Balkh Bastan

He pockets his *kippah* before
entering his café,
where the metal chairs no longer
fill with foreigners & soldiers.

Descending the stained stairs,
he unlocks the storage room,
flicks on the fan & warms
one of the five stoves.

The green walls creak & ache
with time. He wipes the skewers
& readies the space
for the Muslim cooks.

The kebab café will soon shut down.
The city's hotels are hollow.
The caterers call less. Everyone is scared
to leave their home.

He stays in his homeland,
reads from the country's last Torah
stored in a brown box
under his bed.

The Liberal Media Made Me Do It

He prays alone, eats alone,
lives alone. Zablon Simintov
will never leave
the last *shul* in Kabul,

where he displays dog-eared
posters, dust-coated books,
& an unused *shofar*
on one of the few places

not covered with black grime.
Tomorrow, on Flower Street,
he'll wipe the fluted-iron door
laden with *Magen Davids*—

under a depilated dome,
the last Jew of Afghanistan hopes
the valley will once again
bloom stars.

M.E. Silverman

Often I get inspiration for poems from simply listening to NPR, BBC, and PBS. One can hear real stories that are poetic truths and almost surreal if one just listens. For example, I first heard about Bao Xishun, the world's tallest man at 8 feet with the longest arms when he reached into two dolphins to pull out plastic from their stomachs in 2006. It seems so fantastic and the out of ordinariness speaks to us because of the heroic act.

The Herdsman & the Dolphin

Fushun Aquarium, China, 2006

He tries not to look as two men in lab coats hold open the
dolphin's jaw, and together, like a giant W, an unnatural
wishing bone, they wait for Bao, the man with the longest
arms in the world, to reach in as far as he can, to immerse
his arm into the slick cave the color of slush and summer dusk.

He really does want to help, to remove the busted balloons
caught in its stomach. Blessed with long arms and eight feet
of height, what does a herdsmen know but the breath of
flowers and the love of wind? With his back to the scientists
and their equipment of blips, monitors for the patient, and
everyone in their crisp masks, he watches spiderweb frost
spread on the window, imprinting his breath, a series of
waves that fades before he even finishes.

While he hesitates to do this task, wondering what its long
mouth will feel like, the wind forces one of the evergreens
to bend against the building, a swift scratching at the pane,
an unrythmical tap on the window that separates him
from a parking lot, a few select observers standing outside
and an overcast sky like a bottomless well.

M.E. Silverman

The Liberal Media Made Me Do It

NPR blogs would completely fail to mention that Trocmé, the subject of this poem, was a Christian and pastor who inspired his rural flock to commit innumerable acts of heroism. That sort of thing is generally beyond their concern. But for a person of faith, the final couplet's question has an answer.

André Trocmé

The child who saw his mother die became a man of God who inspired and led the people of Le Chambon, and "who refused to turn Jewish refugees over to the Nazis during the occupation, who defied them openly, to their faces, even when he was under arrest"
—Krulwich Wonders, NPR blog

Because she was tossed from the car,
You ran and looked and drank the black
Of things that are and things that are
Not—and then the world was lack

And nothingness. You never could
Turn from your mother's staring face
Or close eyes gone as still as wood.
You braved the borderlands, a place

Of wandering, where rivers kept
Floating her form away from you.
Though others sang, *Accept, accept,*
Stark courage was what led you through.

Who knew your bravery would save
So many from the fire and grave?

Marly Youmans

The Liberal Media Made Me Do It

As I recall, astronaut Karl Henize's wife, Caroline Henize, was being interviewed by NPR about her husband, who had made news headlines as the "oldest American in space." Karl Henize was 40 years old when he applied to NASA, and he went on a space mission some years later.

The Three Dreams of Karl Henize

*He had three dreams: marriage and a family,
to be like Buck Rogers, and
to climb Mount Everest.*
—Caroline Henize on NPR, 10/15/93

I remember white lilies and hyacinths
lighting the aisle you walked down to marry me,
and hushed whispers of our guests,
expectant as buds in springtime.
I focused on those flowers, each petal
a guide to keep my thoughts from tumbling
down the scree slope of fear.

When you gave birth, our wakefulness led
to quiet conversations at dawn,
and we marveled at the blooming
of that tiny red bud,
the channeled head of our firstborn.

Two sons, two daughters now.
I walk the house at midnight, watching
disks of moonlight through the windows,
and the pale beauty of dreaming faces,
avalanche lilies in a heathered meadow.

* * *

Heather buds smothered by first snow,
many people's dreams bloomed
briefly, faded and fell to earth.
From an asteroid's blue glow
burning through smudged comic pages,
my ambition took spark.

The Liberal Media Made Me Do It

Imagining the jazzy tights and thigh
high boots that Buck and Wilma wore,
I applied, at forty, to NASA's space program.
Laughter from people bereft of dreams
mingled in my ears with the surge of rockets
lifting me toward dark gardens.

"Oldest American in Space," said the headlines
when, eighteen years later, Buck's memory and I
traversed the vast black
waterfall spilling its crystal star flowers
fragrant with jet fuel, and fear.

* * *

Wearing a down parka over wool surplus pants,
Mount Everest strode up to our front door.
The brass knocker dropped like an ice hammer
clattering down a crevasse.
When a dream comes knocking,
you have to go. I packed my bags for Kathmandu.

Now, the weeks spent running up stairs
wearing a fifty-pound pack propel me,
as we transport loads from base camp up
and up through the avalanche lilies,
to zones where the squished
aster shapes in compressed ice gleam
under a thousand years of weight.

My brain whirls. My lungs press
against the edges of this galaxy
where higher is not high enough,
and I feel the burst
of red oxygen buds
splattered over snow,
geranium petals flung
under the Milky Way.

Sheryl Clough
— *First published in* Soundings Review.

I'm a music lover, but I had never heard of Blossom Dearie until I learned about her death on NPR in February 2009. I immediately did some research on her, and was inspired to write this poem.

One story on her can be found at: http://www.npr.org/templates/story/story.php?storyId=100471291

Remembering Blossom Dearie

April 28, 1926 – February 7, 2009

So, here I am at the Skylark Club, a machinist
from Hoboken itching for a one-night stand
in the city, and I suggest we get some drinks
after the show, chew the fat until the bar closes.

I pretend to know something about the tonality
of a song, but she's talking about Manhattan, how it's
a soulful place, stirs up the music inside her,
how sometimes it makes her mad. She prefers

Paris. When she speaks to me with that pixie voice,
I assume that she wants me, but she's not interested
in sex. Instead, we dance to *When Fools Rush In*,
one of her favorite Johnny Mercer tunes.

Because I'm not used to rejection, I ask
her again to go home with me. All she does
is light a cigarette and begin to hum, as if to say,
Easy now buster, my name is Blossom.

Nina Soifer
—*Originally appeared in the 2009 issue of* Hotmetalpress.net.

I wrote this poem after listening to the Libyan writer, Hisham Matar on
Fresh Air with Terry Gross on April 2, 2013. Mr. Matar's father had been a
political prisoner in Libya—along with other male members of his family—
for opposing the Qaddafi regime, and was eventually executed. Hisham Matar
said that his father, throughout his life, memorized poetry, and while in prison,
recited the poems to fellow prisoners. When Hisham was a child, his father
told him that memorizing poetry was "like carrying a house in your chest."

House of Poems

I have no food nor drink

but I carry a million words

that lie down with me as I sleep

and wake raising my house

letter by letter

Donna Decker

I listen to and watch a full range of public media, including KCRW and watch KCET, in Santa Monica, though lately I've been watching KLCS or KDOC. The story that inspired this could have surfaced on any of these.

Now I Am Nothing

The old man speaks of
His days walking the wire
A wire dancer he calls it
But now he is old and washed up
He can only teach children how to tempt fate

"Now I am nothing" he says

I too know this resignation
Once I held a hammer
I built things
Repaired things
Brought joy to other people's lives
I was "unskilled" labor - blue collar
Working poor
But now I am just poor
I am defined by my birthdate
I am a medical statistic
Once I railed against
The medical business
But that was when I still thought
I could walk away
When I thought I didn't need them
Now I know I do need them
Need their pills and their needles
Their hospitals and doctors

The Liberal Media Made Me Do It

So today while I was in Rite aid
Getting some things I had a
Strange moment of clarity
It was in the liquor aisle…
All those bottles of Vodka
The means for my escape
Laid out before me
And it meant nothing
Nothing at all

A wind of great sadness blew through my soul
I wished it would pick me up and carry me far away from here
That's when I realized – when I knew it couldn't
Because

Now I am nothing

RD Armstrong

Happiness

After a Speech by behavioral economist, Daniel Kahneman on TED Radio Hour, Nov. 30, 2013

I've heard that every memory
is a reconstruction, a product
of the storytelling self
and that a feeling counts
only in retrospect,
never in the moment.

How then to think about
the image I have screened forever
in that most exclusive
theater of my memory?
Sunlight seeps through lowered
blinds as I lie in my crib.
Nearby, a radio plays.
I can still hum the song.
I've identified and placed it
in the year after my birth.

In the memory, the song
pulses with light, the streaks
of afternoon grow longer
as I watch, apart
yet part of all that I perceive.
Is this reconstruction?
I prefer to think it happened,
is happening now, will always
happen, this early vision
of happiness, the only
paradise we ever know.

Robbi Nester

"Poem on a Line by Anne Sexton" came from notes I was taking when I was driving down interstate 81 from my home in Pennsylvania en route to the Virginia Center for the Creative Arts (The VCCA) in Amherst, VA. I don't know what station I was listening to, just that I was scanning the left hand side of the dial, hoping to find NPR. This phrase jumped out at me, and I wrote it in my notebook, not a small feat, as I drive a stick shift vehicle. Whenever I travel, I try to find an NPR station. When I hear, say, Cokie Roberts or Marty Moss-Cowane, I feel like I'm accompanied by friends.

Poem on a Line by Anne Sexton, "We are all writing God's poem."

Today, the sky's the soft blue of a work shirt washed a thousand times.
The journey of a thousand miles begins with a single step.
On the interstate listening to NPR, I heard a Hubble scientist
say, "The universe is not only stranger than we think,
it's stranger than we *can* think."
I think I've driven into spring, as the woods revive
with a loud shout, redbud trees, their gaudy scarves
flung over bark's bare limbs.
Barely doing sixty, I pass a tractor trailer called
Glory Bound, and aren't we just?
Just yesterday, I read Li Po: "There is no end of things in the heart,"
but it seems like things are always ending—vacation
or childhood, relationships, stores going out of business,
like the one that sold jeans that really fit—
And where do we fit in? How can we get up
in the morning, knowing what we do?
But we do, put one foot after the other, open the window,
make coffee, watch the steam curl up and disappear.
At night, the scent of phlox curls in the open window,
while the sky turns red violet, lavender, thistle,
a box of spilled crayons. The moon
spills its milk on the black tabletop for the thousandth time.

Barbara Crooker
—*First published in Margie*

Although I didn't write it down, I believe "The Stock Market Loses Fluidity" came from listening to Marketplace, *via station WHHY, Philadelphia (90.1). I listen to them while I'm making dinner, while I listen to my local NPR station, WDIY (88.1), Bethlehem, PA in the morning, and alternative music NPR station WXPN (88.5), Philadelphia, at random moments during the day when I'm cooking or cleaning. I not only feel like all three stations are part of my household, but I put my money where my ears are, and support them, too.*

THE STOCK MARKET LOSES FLUIDITY
2008 NPR headline

I'll show you what's *really* liquid—it's this sunlight pouring down
from the west, from the great glass jar of the sky. The creek playing
its little tune, running over the stones. The descant of syllables
in the mockingbird's song. For not a single hickory nut
banked by the squirrels will gain any interest.
Not a grain of wheat in the wallet of a chipmunk's cheek
will increase in worth. The bear's fat layer is its IRA.
Here in the woods, it's autumn's great investment portfolio; look,
everything's turned the color of money: copper, brass, gold.

Barbara Crooker
—*First published in* Switched-On Gutenberg

The Liberal Media Made Me Do It

This poem was inspired by a story about a chimpanzee named Lucy and her human counterpart Janis Carter.

Lucy

I'm embossing paper, punching out leaves
and petals, while listening to podcasts, letting
them play, not choosing a *Radiolab* topic.
This episode is about a chimp raised as a child,

called *daughter* by her caretakers and their family
until she grew too big and sexually mature. Too
violent to be contained, worse than human teens.
A few minutes in, I remember this story
and its sad ending, but can't advance the track.

Stuck, like people who gawk at a gory accident,
or click on photos that come with a warning:
Disturbing. Explicit! I continue to listen,
punch paper borders for cards, remember to breathe.

This time, I think more of Lucy, expected
to learn how to live in the jungle with other chimps,
instead of a house, where she made tea for guests.
I rise to go to the website, look for the final photo
snapped of Lucy hugging Janice Carter, the woman

who had stayed in the Gambian jungle to help her adapt.
Janice signed, "Lucy, go!"
Lucy signed back, "No. Come!"
Three years for Janice, in her own cage on the island
to keep the chimps from stealing her cookware, food.

A year after that photo, Lucy's skeleton was found,
no skin or hair nearby, her hands and feet cut off,
hands that had signed, made tea. Too trusting
of humans, she likely greeted her poacher,
perhaps hoped it was Janice returned.

Lucy is the also name given a hominid fossil.
DNA in her mitochondria says she's our mother.
With no one to hug, I go to the kitchen to make tea.

Joan Mazza

The Liberal Media Made Me Do It

From: All Things Considered, "Spouses on the Campaign Trail,"
October 17, 2007

Radio Interview

Ann Romney's missionary voice beams from some NPR studio across inaccessible stars and blue-black space while I drive on in the coming dark, anxious to arrive home before my vision fades, before my leg brace constricts my calf, before spasms. She crows—*I have no MS symptoms and haven't for years* – and credits rest, healthy meals, acupuncture, and reflexology for her symptom-free life. Why, she feels *protected* from that evil, eating fruit and whole grains and resting with her feet up on a cushion (*Sometimes she just HAS to stop and rest*), while I grimace and regret the ice cream, rue the wine, lament those missed naps. No daily or weekly shots for her; steroids are hideous and the hope of stem cells? (*Stem cells* – uttered like a loathsome curse.) Well, she hopes research halts *before any more innocent lives are taken in the name of science*. I envision her heeled shoes winking as her rose-tipped toes slip in before she launches back home to ride Baron, her show horse. (*Riding fights fatigue and stress.*) Then I am yelling at the radio, pounding the steering wheel at that nail-driven-home voice so much like the roaring page, the bastard blues – I want to propel Baron through an unlatched gate, his tail a free flag in the wind, push that smiling voice down a flight of stone steps until those fancy shoes fly, and punch my hand through her smug assumption that she knows exactly how to manage MS, never acknowledging that my MS might be a different animal all together. Lights on our cedar trees appear and disappear in the growing wind. I turn onto our gravel driveway, silence the car, clamber awkwardly out, stand supported by my quad cane and leg brace, and admit that I so desperately want, oh how I want, oh, oh, with my heart in my mouth, oh, how I want to be her.

Marie Kane
—*Appeared previously in her book,* Their Buoyant Bodies Respond *(Pittsburgh: Inglis Poetry House, 2010).*

The Liberal Media Made Me Do It

This poem was inspired by a Frontline *program, "League of Denial: The NFL's Concussion Crisis," first aired on October 8, 2013.*

A Retired Athlete

I worked in the trenches with my brother grunts,
the blue-collar guys opening holes
for the glamour boys to run through.
O-line grinders like me never got the credit
we deserved, though we feasted on thousand-dollar
dinners and whores, like everyone else in that fantasyland
of Monopoly money. We were millionaires
working for billionaires who'd built a world
separate from the one where fans worshipping us
scratched and clawed to pay their bills. That orgy
of fame and glory was some sweet lobotomy.

Then I heard the whispers: "He's lost
his explosion off the snap. He used to blow up
D-lines at the point of attack, but now he's just bombing.
He's lost his punch, his pop, his killer instinct,
his pride. He's a dying lion out there,
  eaten up by opponents he used to maul.
It's painful to watch." My body, which carried me
out of poverty, had been whispering the same thing.
I didn't listen, refused to hear, until my body
shouted so loud
I could hear nothing else beyond the pain.

The Liberal Media Made Me Do It

I'm a war hero who won his Purple Heart
playing a child's game. I lived
in the fawning light of the camera's eye, gaining
game-show glory on the televised battlefield.
Concussions and devil's-bargain drugs, one
busted marriage and two busted knees....
Was it all worth it? I don't know. I wanted
it to go on forever, and, like a fool,
thought it would. But time called
an audible on me. Now,
middle age barely begun, I hobble through
this cold jungle, shrouded in an obscurity
that feels like the darkness to come.

Richard Hamwi

This poem was inspired by the American Masters *episode on Quincy Jones.*

Aubade with a Quincy Jones Biography on PBS

In response to Pound's "The Garret"

Dawn came in like Philip Marlowe
drunk on rye and gray with stubble.
You called in sick and I took you

to the pharmacy. Michael asked,
"How's your wife?" ringing up your drugs.
You've never told him that I'm not

your wife. The Texas Family Code,
line 2.401, declares
we're married if we represent

to others that we're married (check),
we live together (check), and we
agree to be married.

Between aneurysms, Quincy
and his girlfriend from the *Mod Squad*
married so she'd gain legal rights

to his remains, her grip of him
wouldn't cremate in the L.A.
County Morgue. Come, let us pity

The Liberal Media Made Me Do It

the married and the unmarried.
He didn't die either time, but
I turn from the TV to look

at dear you, neither my husband nor
my unhusband, eyes glazed over
like cakes.

I dole your dose and brew your tea.
Yes, life has something better than this
hour of waking together: this power

To guarantee your body lies
With me till I say otherwise.

Barbara Duffey

The Liberal Media Made Me Do It

I heard this particular Writers Almanac *segment in December of 2008 on WABE, 90.1, in Atlanta.*

In the Depths of the Recession

I'm reduced to crawling in an attic,
sealing squirrel holes for a tough customer -
 I don't want to see any daylight up there!
And my paint-spattered radio's going
with first Brahms then *The Writer's Almanac*
as I soldier-squirm through insulation,
dragging flashing to screw over fascia
gaps ringed by gnaw marks which is when
I hear that today's poem is by Cecilia.
Cecilia! We critiqued work all last fall
around that table, sometimes with wine.
We stayed up late election night, toasting.
And now, in these lines, she's on a Prague bridge,
lost in thought, looking down, when a man
approaches, says, *Don't jump,* before he
proposes marriage on the spot.
You can tell old Garrison likes that line.
I've stopped squirming to listen, to push
aside a long-dead rat in its last trap.

But don't worry, this is not a lament
that her words put girdles round the world
while I'm up here with skeletal remains,
warring with creatures who won't fight fair.
She has chosen her bridge, I my attic
where I'm nodding along as always to,
 Stay in touch and do good work
when I see sunlight pinholing its way
through two more gaps in the far-corner eaves.
And as I'm grunting my way over there
(to do good work) I'm thinking of Kipling
on his just-announced birthday, how I'd
memorized *If* in the sixth grade with its
caution against coveting others' lives.
Or did it? I can't remember. I'm crawling.

Rupert Fike

Pale Blue Dot

Candice Hansen-Koharcheck, I'm not sure how
to pronounce your name, but you were the first

to spot it, this two-pixel speck otherwise known
as planet Earth. Sitting at your screen, shades drawn,

office dark, you searched the digital photos sent back
by Voyager 1, four billion miles from your desk.

And there it was, not the big blue marble swirling
with clouds and continents, not the one Apollo astronauts

the sheer beauty brought tears—thanking God and America,
declaring no need to fight over borders or oil; this was not

that view; this was how our planet might look to an alien.
And yet how close this photo came to not being taken at all—

scientists arguing, aiming the camera back at the sun
might fry the lens, questioning the worth of such a risk,

this shot you say still gives you chills, dear Candice,
our planet bathed in the spacecraft's reflective light.

Pale blue dot lit by a glowing beam: I'm surprised
Christians didn't have a hey-day, though viewing

His crowning achievement requires squinting.
When NASA put it on display at the Jet Propulsion Lab,

a blow-up print spanning fourteen feet, visitors touched
the pinprick so often the image needed constant replacing,

perhaps because without the little arrow we wouldn't know
which pinprick was home. And yet its barely-there-ness

The Liberal Media Made Me Do It

doesn't excuse the plastic bags, duct tape, juice packs,
sweat pants that lodge in the stomachs of whales. And yet

its lack of distinction doesn't pardon the brown-pudding goop
on the Gulf of Mexico's floor, a goop in which nothing alive

has been found. To reckon that speck, mourn the loss
of the black torrent toad. To take it in, grasp its full weight,

then turn toward a child's insistent *give me a ride in a rocket ship!*
With meteors and turbulence! Like you, dear Candice, alone

and in the dark while a loved one's asking *Where are you going?*
When are you coming back?

Martha Silano

To Be Continued

After a radio documentary, Walking Out of History, aired on KPCC FM

Today is not the end of the world.
In the pantry, a white
splinter of onion like a narwhal
charting its arctic course
twists toward the light.

I think of stout Shackleton
 and his Endurance,
how he crossed Antarctica
but lost his ship in 1914.
A world bereft of color
where the eyes starved
and the body too.

How did they spend
two years adrift on ice,
given up for lost,
to return at last,
as though Odysseus
had come again to Ithaca
with all his crew?
The frozen ocean took
 almost a year to upend
the wooden ship, last of its kind.
They packed their stores
in lifeboats that would be
their world, taking the heavy
photographic plates,
our record of those years.

The Liberal Media Made Me Do It

For all the loneliness,
they never were alone.
A pod of orca in pursuit
of seals once tore through
ice, encountered them—
no doubt in mutual surprise.
Emperor Penguins shuffled
across ice fields, eggs
balanced on their feet.

Sometimes the sun would
rise and set three times
before the end of day, if
ending has a meaning in this place.
And all the elements that had
seemed kind conspired to kill.
Even spring, melting the floes
that served them for a home,
turned loose what they deemed
solid, making each step
likely to become their last.
The Southern Lights must
have rung the stars with its
magnetic charge, but
did they even hear that, nestled
deep inside their fur-lined bags?

There is no easy ending.
The world goes on and on,
and somewhere, even now,
new worlds are being born
or found or made. Deep in space
or in the body's fastness,
or freed from under ice.

Robbi Nester

The Liberal Media Made Me Do It

The inspiration for this poem came from Science Friday *(NPR). It aired March 8, 2013.*

The Inheritors

Here for a micro-tick of the likely timeless clock, I consider
the multitudes that no longer exist and ones that still may
in the near and far future. Will the cockroach
persist, its longevity rival that of the dinosaur? Might life
remake itself from the tough and aggressive ant? Perhaps
the most fierce or single-minded won't, on this
altered planet, be the one to endure when the next worst
catastrophe plays out: no powerful jolt from a meteor,
but a slower process, rising and falling temperatures, subtle
toxins, genetic splice and drift, sporadic local blight.

Of course I cheer on the ones with the larger brains. But if the meek
are to inherit, how likely my kind? And if one more humble
is destined to reign, it could be the lichen-loving tardigrade.
An extremophile, this roly poly thing (called water bear and moss
piglet for its shape) can hibernate (enter its tun state) to withstand
and revive from boiling, massive radiation, one degrees Kelvin,
a year of desiccation, the vacuum of space.

Struggling in its constricted droplet of water
beneath the magnifying lens, it works eight legs with miniscule
claws, its brain invisible but present, its future not yet fixed. And I
make a wish: may it continue. Having left behind
all near-relatives, may it stay on that divergent path
and prosper, develop greater generosity than us, as well as
a broader understanding, even wisdom. May its progeny

and its progeny's progeny never believe themselves the chosen,
blessed among all forms. If we perish, may it
survive, multiply, replenish this world, or another. May some
yet-to-be being reach a higher state so that
if such a thing be possible, the new age it brings forth
will know a peace we have not.

Lavina Blossom

The content was sparked by a story aired on Morning Edition *on Dec. 31, 2013, called "Nothing Focuses the Mind Like the Ultimate Deadline: Death." The story was about a new watch created by a Swedish man that can be set to count down the days to one's hypothetical death (based on life expectancy data) .... with the belief that it will make the wearer live life more fully. However, the researchers discovered that for many people, the watch can produce negative and even dangerous results.*

Strap a Tikker Onto Your Wrist, Stretch Your Arm To Heaven

Nothing focuses the mind like
the ultimate deadline.

Set the happiness watch
for twenty years –
long enough to have a new career,
write a book, run for mayor.
Ten years –
travel the world, keep a photo blog,
grow herbs, learn to cook.
Five years – two –
ditch the diet, skydive into
the Grand Canyon, leave
a giant footprint, donate blood.
Go see everyone you've ever known.

Reach for what matters, the watch
reminds you again and again.

The Liberal Media Made Me Do It

Or instead, you may
become paralyzed with fear.
Begin to hate your neighbors,
be annoyed by every lame-brained
driver and rainy day, find doctors
worthless, books a total waste of time.
That dark underbelly – anxiety –
casts a shadow on the glory you felt
when the chains fell away.

Hurl the thing at the wall –
convince yourself you're still immortal.

And why not? No inventor
has the goods on you. Better to stay
numb, race toward the weekend,
watch TV. Believe in exercise,
wine, the need for more vitamin D.
You'd rather be the poor schmuck
who gets hit next week by a bus
and goes down smiling, oblivious.

Kate Hutchinson

"Near Misses" was written after the large hurricanes predicted to hit us, but missed: David, Florence, Floyd, etc. Since moving to South Florida in 1975, I have experienced only two major hurricanes, one of which (Wilma in 2005) really affected my area, and Andrew in 1992 which devastated south Miami. Irene (one of the non-wind hurricanes) flooded our area, but no wind damage. I wrote the poem based on the stress and tension of just hearing about them and the relief of their passing us by. It was based on an article on NPR regarding people who don't heed the call to evacuate in an approaching hurricane (1998).

Near Misses

Perhaps it's about hurricanes
that graze by once every few years,
those who are spared angered by relief,
adopting complacency as a badge—
not a good sign.

Or danger—
the thrill of speed,
the natural high of fear.
Look at anyone's cheeks: how pink!
And the eyes fevered and glassy.

But then again—perhaps it's just love:
the silken strands around the throat,
the skipped beat in time to the phone,
the sense of floating in the dark,
the loss of self when tethers break.

Barbra Nightingale

The Liberal Media Made Me Do It

This poem was inspired by a story I heard on NPR about Project X-Ray, which must have aired in the spring of 2005. It would have been on All Things Considered, *I think.*

The Bats of Carlsbad Caverns Ponder Their Ancestors

The infamous World War II Brave Bomber Bats
of White Sands, New Mexico, strapped to cans of napalm
and trained to ignite Tokyo. These bomber bats escaped

their pens and exploded the General's Nash Ambassador sedan,
so the plan of attack was abandoned and the remaining bats
sacked. They flew away over the once-white desert sand,

now burned to blue-green glass from the heat of the first
atomic bomb's explosion. Without work, they left the missile range,
migrating to the Caverns, where they practiced their low-flight

maneuvers on the Park's patrons. The bats still bore
the singed back fur that marked their work as animals of war,
and their blackness absorbed the beauty of the crystal sunsets

in the Caverns, whose ceilings and floors reached out to one another,
to eat up the nothing between them, while the bats swarmed
in silhouetted flight patterns at dusk, enjoying rest,

except that the bomb had gone off a few hundred miles away.
They watched their shadows skirr across the desiccated ground
whose own atoms' nuclei were itching to split.

Barbara Duffey

The Liberal Media Made Me Do It

This poem was inspired by a story on The Splendid Table *in which a beekeeper related his recipe for mead, using a whole hive of live bees.*

Making Whole Hive Mead

The hive was dying anyhow:
the queen laid only sterile eggs,
 though scouts still scanned the fields
for purple beesbread,
almond trees in bloom.
The workers kept carving out
their perfect hexagons, marble-white
cathedrals filled with golden light.
So veiled and suited, we first
boiled the water in a cast iron pot,
then caught the bees up in a smoky
stupor, hive humming
like a chapel full of monks.
Too stunned to even swarm,
they kept their posts, fanning
the queen, who barely stirred.
On our knees before the hive,
we paid her court, lifted out
the frames, emptying the hive,
honey, bees and all,
into the pot, a catastrophe
of broken bodies, melting wax.
We kept on crushing corpses
with a spoon, until the cloudy brew
had cleared to amber, tasting
of summer fields, but with a sting.
We raised our cups like lords, and drank
to time and fermentation, bringing
everything at last to proper sweetness.

Robbi Nester

The Liberal Media Made Me Do It

I heard "A Farm-to-Table Delicacy from Spain: Roasted Baby Pig" on NPR, September 4, 2013, and sure enough dreamed a strange dream that night.
  A print version of it can be found here: http://www.npr.org/blogs/thesalt/2013/09/04/218959923/a-farm-to-table-delicacy-from-spain-roasted-baby-pig

Roast Suckling Pig

Driving home from the gynecologist, after my yearly exam,
I hear about Spanish festival food on NPR: month-old piglet nurslings,
carefully safeguarded from germs, fed nothing
but their mother's milk, then plucked from the sow's teats,
slaughtered and trucked in a couple hours to Madrid, so diners
can devour crisp-skinned deliciousness only one or two days
dead.
      I picture butterflied baby, ears perked, eyes glazed,
sliding—grinning snout first—onto Hemingway's plate.
And it's not that I would resist a piece, cut up and served
(head and hooves removed to the kitchen, thank you very much).

But that night I dream we are roasting iguanas—which we never
have or would eat—in a slow oven, belly up,
on a bed of greens. After a quarter-hour,
when we pull out the pan to baste, they look up
with startlingly blue round eyes—
both at the front of their heads—as they recline
splayed out like my dog, who wants some air
on her privates, or a belly rub.

Judy Kronenfeld

The following blurb comes from a story on All Things Considered, *in which the journalist considers the history of the origins of the foundling wheel: "In 1198, Pope Innocent III was dismayed by the number of newborns caught in the nets of fishermen on the Tiber River. He ordered the first Medieval "foundling wheel" — a rotating platform located in the wall of a church that allowed women to anonymously leave their newborns." During this time, my partner and I were taking steps that eventually led to the adoption of our older son in 2008.*

The story can be found at http://www.npr.org/templates/story/story.php?storyId=7730566

The Foundling Wheel

i.
They swept the river, caught the dead
in nets. Then a wheel with a box
let someone leave a child. As boats sway
beneath the wall, their loose cords

swing and clank the hollow masts,
so the masts call out like dulled bells.
At low tide, their hulls lie in mud.
A mother rolls her stroller back and forth,

looking at—the rain? My mind drifts at night,
the current rising on the bank,
the sound of water splashing from the roof.

The blue curtain glows at dawn.
I hear the gulls and don't sleep well.

The Liberal Media Made Me Do It

ii.
The one who set her son adrift
must have stood among the reeds
as long she could. The hand that throws
the stone recalls its weight.

A father's body changes, too,
on a molecular level:
a small disturbance among fallen leaves,
a soft thud. A stream of light

at dawn, the bells ring and ring,
the world's wheel turning toward
this, the 6th day of October:

the child sleeps beside our bed
and you make toast with red plum jam.

Blas Falconer

The Liberal Media Made Me Do It

This poem was the result of an interview I heard when Laura Flanders used to host KALW's Your Call *in San Francisco, circa 2001-2004.*

Dead Air

Today's phone-in topic was public art
and its social role, but the dispirited
caller had given up graffiti, since
she didn't believe in spray cans
and *never found the right felt-tip marker.*
My old desk radio was turning
into one of Dali's clocks.
Surely this voice was clinically
depressed before it lost faith
in aerosols. It sat on the ear,
the air, like a slab of bad cheese.
The pushy English host and her guests
were exchanging nervous glances, audible
from the shifts of their ergonomic chairs,
such imperative to lose this woman
without apparent cruelty, fast.
Someone must have fumbled for the right
switch, the digital heave-ho, the polite
sidestep, *so glad you brought that up—*
and missed: what followed was ten
seconds of Line Two's sad breathing:
This is how a person who can't paint,
someone with a hook in the heart, sounds.
Here is the wind whistling through
that particular canyon. And it's live.

Julie Bruck
*—Originally published in her third collection,
   MONKEY RANCH (Brick Books, 2012).*

This poem originated from a story on Morning Edition, *January 15, 2012, and is the current working title poem of my manuscript.*

Belonging

I had no doubt, no doubt at all that is a Stradivarius ...
it was so beautiful, so very beautiful.
— Bernard Greenhouse, the Countess of Stainlein

I was of a different world.
Crucial to harmony, but never real.
I came alive

and learned to be held.
My back and neck in concert
with your fingers.

I had never known belonging.
We filled the air around us
and everyone who heard us knew.

You restored me.
It took years, but I was restored.
I forgot my history then:

Trash bound, mistaken.
Authenticity always in question.
I couldn't hear past: before or beyond.

I came to believe you made me real.
I learned to live
and to be put away.

Jennifer Flescher

This poem is based on a segment of Radiolab *called "Rippin' the Rainbow a New One" from the* Colors *episode. I listened to a podcast of the episode, which originally aired on May 21, 2012.* Radiolab *is a melding of science and art, and the hosts often use metaphors to explain or illustrate concepts. This show used a choir singing a sixteen note chord to illustrate what it might be like to see a larger color spectrum. I'm a singer, so this metaphor fascinated me. That sound, along with some fascinating facts about a sea creature with incredible color vision, got this poem off the ground.*

Radiolab: **Colors**

The choir sings a sixteen note chord, so bright it stings
the eyes and throat, notes more colors than the eye can discern,
but the ear can hold, for seconds at a time, the extended flash.

Colors carry memory, the exact purple of the French lilacs
against the shocking white of a late May snow, how the frost
edged the tiny blossoms with an iridescent glass; the orange
hunting jacket you wore when we ran outside
to catch the snowflakes on our tongues; the sepia brown
of your eyes when we pressed our noses close.

Colors evaporate as quickly as passing notes,
but memory is the sky that holds color together,
turns water vapor into a spectrum, a promise,
a mirage just a few feet out of reach.

Kris Bigalk

The Liberal Media Made Me Do It

This poem was inspired by a story that aired on Morning Edition *(NPR-WNYC-FM in New York City), on 10/15/13, about the Indian Bottom association of church singers in Appalachia. They have no notated songbook but have preserved the style of church singing prominent in the 17th Century.*

Folklore: Practice and Theory

The voices come through the paradox of the periphery
at 6:55 a.m. and the theory that what is unalloyed has
the better memory: of how to mourn the stars and their
dusk blood force, long since surrendered to the cities;
of how to mourn the toll the earth exacts for humble
comforts, shelter and warmth, and for entering it
through an unnatural egress. They might recall the smell
of days when the air is as starched as an Easter dress
and the water is clear from flame and silt; because
in poverty and despair, there is no cause and effect.
These are voices that know the distance between
where a man says he has become the person he always
wanted to be, and where that same man jumps off
a building. For me, that is about twenty years.
For the voices, it is the sum of the ages.

Jane Rosenberg LaForge

The Liberal Media Made Me Do It

I'm in Kalamazoo, Michigan, and my station is WMUK, bless 'em. The story which comes from an anecdote I heard on the show Performance Today, *is nearly all there in the poem.*

Staccato

Stravinski was famous
for his staccato. Ormandy
said "Stravinsky – bup, bup, bup, bup.
   He's dead, poor guy.
   Play it legato." But

today forsythia raises
its batons all over town.
Ormandy's dead, poor guy,
   and every branch
   is staccato with buds —
   bup, bup, bup, bup.

Susan Blackwell Ramsey

Three Public Radio Haikus

Performance Today

Another texter
on the road. I want to ram
her. Wait! Debussy!

Morning Edition

You're so serious.
Really. Way too serious.
More Britney Spears.

Live from the Met

Even if they sang
in English, I would still need
popcorn and footnotes.

Elizabeth Kerlikowske

The Liberal Media Made Me Do It

The two stories I used are from different newscasts, "Octopus Trix," on All Things Considered, *Dec. 6, 1997, and "Clara Barton," on* Weekend Edition, *Dec. 7, 1997*

Proofs

Heartbeat + Caffeine = Hyperbole
Or: Heart + Caffeine = Access to Restricted Areas.

In the news today, Clara Barton's untouched
Missing Soldiers Office found preserved, full of inexplicable bolts
of black fabric. Then they discover a photograph:

the black swagged out the windows
for Lincoln's funeral procession.

Also: octopi can be taught
to open jars of food. If the lid
is too tight, they strain, turn red,
eyes bulging, using four tentacles.

Heart + News + Caffeine = What do these things weigh

together, what do they weigh?

The soldiers' mothers' searching . . .

Clara making lists, accounting for the numbers of the dead,

the historians mystified by the voluminous
cloth, solving for X:

the procession, the funeral of the commander–

All that faith and effort, like the octopus

so satisfied and smart with his open jar . . .

The solution is always a nourishment in itself.

Sally Ball
—from Annus Mirabilis *(Barrow Street, 2005)*

My local NPR station is Jefferson Public Radio, JPR, in Ashland, Oregon but I actually saw this article on the website. "For Day Trader, Losing $20,000 Just Part Of The Job."

A look at a direct access trading firm day trader. The article focuses on a single trade on a fertilizer company after the trader sees a press release stating that the company is cutting production. While tracking with day trading software and charts, he miscalculates the diminishment of the shares and loses $20,000 in one day.

Here's a link to the story:
http://www.npr.org/templates/story/story.php?storyId=102192891

Candlestick Patterns

Definition: In finance, a specifically named candlestick pattern demonstrates a movement in prices of securities or currencies that some believe can predict a particular market movement. NPR Website, March 21, 2009

They're symbols, you know, shorthand
for price, the buy-and-sell at points
in time, and you might look
for a pattern,
a Morning Star maybe, a shift in the wind when
the bulls crash in,
or Abandoned Baby to keep
the bear back,
and think secrets secrets in the red and green bars
with little wicks or
sometimes long, and you must read them,
not like a recipe or even a will,
read them like the last letter from a love soon gone,

The Liberal Media Made Me Do It

look for the sign,
for Dark Cloud Cover
or Hanging Man
and feel the pressure between those that want in
or out,
lean into their need,
think candle, think light,
and if the chart seems choppy,
don't fear, just wait,
listen hard to the story, the one being whispered
as the dollars brush by.

Amy MacLennan

This was inspired by a line in a novel reviewed on All Things Considered.

Fire

From a line in The Sweet Girl, a novel by Annabel Lyon

We must all have fire in us
Breathing out prodigious clouds of smoke
On winter mornings, when the windows frost.

And this goes on for years, as though
Nothing at all were lost.
We must have fire in us.

And where the gangly palms outnumber oaks
Overheated sleepers make a tangle of the sheets
Dreaming of winter mornings when the windows frost.

Who can calculate the cost
Of burning so steadily and long?
We must have fire in us

Or else we'd be reduced to ash and ends
Far sooner than we are.
We must have fire in us
To brave those winter mornings when the windows frost

Robbi Nester
—*Previously published in* The Edwin E. Smith Journal

The Liberal Media Made Me Do It

Prompted by a news story on NPR (KUOW 94.9FM) about a reporter's Irish grandmother who would tell the same stories with different details each time.

Revision

The story reinvents itself
each night around the campfire.
Once in Ireland, for example,
upon a time some terrible storm
left a horse high up in a tree

or if someone lives by the sea,
then a seal. In the highlands,
a goat stands in, regardless
what each has in common:
always a figure which has lost

its spot in the appropriate world,
erased by chance or embellishment.
And when the wind blows through
the treetops, a baby and cradle fall
out of one version and into another.

This tree might burst into flames
at any moment or be felled by an ax
wishing to carve more of its kind.
The story, though, goes on and on,
unafraid, untouched but changed.

Allen Braden
—*Previously published in* The Bellingham Review.

This poem was inspired by Prairie Home Companion*'s annual joke show.*

Tell Me If You've Heard This One

Surprise is what we value in a joke
we think, a different reason for the chicken
to cross, a deeper basement to the blonde's
bemusement, some new group screwing in a lightbulb,
odder animal walks into a bar,
the final wise word from the patient rabbi.

A priest, a Baptist minister and a rabbi
walk into a bar. Barkeep says "Is this a joke?"
Sure, and a good one, a world where every bar
is just as apt to host a talking chicken
as an ecumenical conference, but no lightbulb
ever flashing on above the blonde.

It's compensation, making fun of blondes,
just like giving the punchline to the rabbi.
The proud are humbled, the oppressed triumph, the lightbulb
goes on – we get it, and laugh. A joke
turns power upside down until a chicken
can be the hero and walk into a bar.

And everyone seems welcome here, bar
none, not just the always-welcome blonde
but those who'd be justified in feeling chicken
about walking in, the solitary rabbi
stranded amid goyim who wouldn't get the jokes
he tells at home, grateful that these lightbulbs

The Liberal Media Made Me Do It

are dim. You'd have to be a pretty dim bulb
not to know that everyone in this bar
has been the butt of the lowest kind of joke,
history's hotfoot, fate's yanked-out chair. Blondes
took over one dark night and riddled the Polaks, the rabbi,
Cletus hazed Rastus, but yo' mama fried that chicken

so good everybody was happy, even the chicken.
It's verbal potluck: Luigi brings a bulb
of garlic, knock-knock the drummer delivers pizza, the rabbi
adds a little schmaltz, everyone in the bar
is flaunting their roots, eventually even the blonde,
The melting pot's a plate, a glass, a joke.

"Rabbi, how many moths to screw in a lightbulb?"
asks the blonde chick at bar, "Only two." "No joke?"
"But like us, you've got to wonder how they got in there."

Susan Blackwell Ramsey
—Reprinted from A Mind Like This *with the permission of the University of Nebraska Press.*

—Sources For The Poems—

The Bird World
Source: "Birds Of A Feather Spy Together, "All Things Considered, Oct. 13, 2013,
http://www.npr.org/2013/10/13/233354052/birds-of-a-feather-spy-together

Technophobia springs from the endless news of endless wars being fought here, there, and everywhere (Syria, Afghanistan, etc.), as well as the increasing Googlization of American society. *http://www.npr.org/templates/story/story.php?storyId=129384107*

The Wiretappers Ball
NPR the two-way 6/17/13 interview with Snowden. *http://www.npr.org/*

Great Fires
The source of this story can be found below.
http://www.npr.org/blogs/thetwo-way/2011/01/18/133026947/

Just You Wait
http://www.wbur.org/npr/165454203/business-news

Into a Void, a Found Poem
Here are the links to the NPR stories that prompted me to write the poem:
http://www.npr.org/2011/04/01/135042915/emergency-reports-detail-slow-mine-blast-response
http://www.npr.org/2011/04/04/135076309/after-w-va-mine-blast-confusion-impeded-search

Boy
http://www.npr.org/2012/03/19/148926698/op-ed-shooting-of-black-teen-reveals-blindness

Fistulated Cow
http://www.radiolab.org/story/197149-holey-cow/

Exchange
One public radio interview on this subject with the scientist can be found at
http://www.ourprg.com/?tag=denise-herzing

Limulus Polyphemus
http://www.npr.org/templates/story/story.php?storyId=1076531

The Trees and the Vines
http://www.npr.org/2013/10/18/237100768/vines-choking-out-trees-in-the-tropics

Writing Blindly
http://www.npr.org/display_pages/features/feature_917851.html

Textile
http://www.npr.org/blogs/money/2013/12/03/247360855/two-sisters-a-small-room-and-the-world-behind-a-t-shirt

Thinning
http://www.npr.org/blogs/health/2013/03/07/173740543/could-a-brain-pacemaker-someday-treat-severe-anorexia

Sonnets for the lost and surviving
http://www.npr.org/2011/09/11/140374672/remembering-the-attacks-of-sept-11 http://www.npr.org/2008/07/22/92616679/identifying-who-survives-disasters-and-why

My Brother's Wandering Soul
http://www.bbc.co.uk/programmes/p00h35lv

Folklore: Practice and Theory
http://www.npr.org/2013/10/15/234606252/before-church-songbooks-there-was-lined-out-singing

Lucy
http://www.radiolab.org/search/?cx=009801551925401469317%3Asrtcvuwcbum&cof=F ORID%3A11&q=lucy&submit=
http://insooutso.tumblr.com/post/504316688/weselec-lucy-chimpanzee-and-janis-carter

Eating in Winter
http://www.uh.edu/engines/epi1036.htm

The Inheritors
http://www.sciencefriday.com/segment/03/08/2013/behold-the-mighty-water-bear.html

Strap a Tikker Onto Your Wrist, Stretch Your Arm To Heaven
http://www.npr.org/blogs/health/2013/12/31/256596253/nothing-focuses-the-mind-like-the-ultimate-deadline-death

The Bats of Carlsbad Caverns Ponder Their Ancestors
http://en.wikipedia.org/wiki/Bat_bomb#cite_note-3

Staccato
http://www.thomasstevensmusic.com/quotablesPage.php?A-Stravinsky-Story-16

Candlestick Patterns
http://www.npr.org/templates/story/story.php?storyId=102192891

—Contributors—

Raised in Ohio, **Martha O. Adams**, author of several books, graduated from Bowling Green State University. She has lived in nine states working as an educator, a mother of four children, retreat leader and as a writer of poetry and non-fiction. She now writes and gardens in Hendersonville, NC. Her most recent book is *What Your Heart Needs to Know* (House of Myrrth, 2008).

RD Armstrong, AKA *Raindog* began his most recent incarnation as a poet in the early 90s. He has 18 chapbooks, 9 books to his name and has been published in nearly 300 poetry magazines, anthologies, blogs and e-zines. He also operates the Lummox Press (celebrating 20 years in 2014) which published the Lummox Journal for 11 years; the Little Red Book series (60 titles) and the new RESPECT series of perfect bound collections of poetry (42 titles). In November, 2012, he began publishing LUMMOX, a new, annual anthology of poetry. He recently began a new "sub-division" called Nine Toes Press. Since 1995, Raindog has labored to serve the world of small press poetry and continues to do so to this day. Visit his website at *www.lummoxpress.com* Raindog is the publisher of this anthology.

Anne Baber has co-authored seven books of non-fiction. Her poetry and fiction have appeared in *Kansas City Voices; Potpourri; I-70 Review; Cuivre River Anthology, Volume V; A Zodiac of Glosas (Ontario Poetry Society); Begin Again: 150 Kansas Poems;* and on the Grammy-Nominated CD *Food for Thought*. Her first poetry Chapbook, *Endless*, was published by Finishing Line Press in 2011. She watches WHYY out of Philadelphia

Sally Ball is the author of *Wreck Me* (2013) and *Annus Mirabilis* (2005), both from Barrow Street Press. Her poems have appeared online at *Narrative* and *Slate*, in print in the *American Poetry Review, Harvard Review, Ploughshares, Yale Review*, and other magazines, as well as in *The Best American Poetry* anthology. An assistant professor of English at Arizona State University, Ball is also associate director of Four Way Books.

Kris Bigalk is the author of the poetry collection *Repeat the Flesh in Numbers* (NYQ Books, 2012); her work has appeared in Poetry City, USA anthologies from Low Brow Press, and in numerous literary magazines, including *Iron Horse Literary Review, Silk Road,* and *Water~Stone Review*. She has won two Minnesota State Arts Board Artist Grants in Poetry, and serves as Director of Creative Writing at Normandale Community College in Bloomington, Minnesota.

Lavina Blossom grew up in rural Michigan. She divides her creative hours between poetry and painting (primarily collage and mixed media). She has an M.F.A. in poetry from the University of California, Irvine, and her poems have appeared in various journals, including The Paris Review, The Literary Review, Kansas Quarterly, as well as in the online journals Poemeleon and 3Elements Review. Her short story "Blue Dog" appeared in the online journal Women Writers. She is an Associate Editor of Poetry for Inlandia: a Literary Journey.

Allen Braden is the author of *A Wreath of Down and Drops of Blood* (University of Georgia) and *Elegy in the Passive Voice* (University of Alaska/Fairbanks). His poems have appeared in textbooks such as *The Bedford Introduction to Literature, Poetry: An Introduction, Literature to Go, Spreading the Word: Editors on Poetry*, and in magazines such as *Virginia Quarterly Review, The New Republic*, and *The Southern Review*. He lives in Lakewood, Washington.

A professor of English and pedagogy, **Kirstin Ruth Bratt** descends from immigrants and maintains an interest in the literature and linguistics of migrant history. In 2013, Kirstin won the Brainerd Writers Alliance fiction contest and was nominated for a Pushcart prize.Her first book of poetry, *These Temples are not in Ruins,* is published by Redbird Press. Her novel, *Ashwak,* is forthcoming from Main Street Rag. Kirsten listens to KNSR 88.9 News / KSJR 90.1 Classical

Julie Bruck is the author of three books of poetry, *Monkey Ranch* (2012*), The End of Travel* (1999), and *The Woman Down-*

stairs (1993). Her work has appeared in such magazines as *Ms, Ploughshares,* and *The New Yorker*, and her awards include two Gold Canadian National Magazine Awards, and the 2012 Governor General's Award for poetry. A former Montrealer, Julie has lived in San Francisco since 1997

A part-time poet and full-time artist working chiefly in mixed media and collage, **Mary Boxley Bullington** has an M.F.A. in Poetry from the University of North Carolina – Greensboro and a doctorate in medieval lit from Indiana University. Her collages and paintings are included in the collections of Virginia Tech, UVA Hospital, and many other private and corporate collections. WBRA, Roanoke, VA is her PBS station.

Sheryl Clough listens to NPR on 88.5 KPLU, broadcast from Seattle/Tacoma Pacific Lutheran University However, at the time she wrote this poem, she lived in Anchorage, AK. The station up there at that time was KUAF . She received her MFA in Creative Writing from the University of Alaska Fairbanks, where she designed and taught UAF's first writing course linked to environmental literature. Her poems, stories and essays have appeared in *Spindrift, Explorations, Storyboard, Sierra, Travelers Tales, Soundings Review* and many others. Sheryl has just edited and published a new anthology, *Through a Distant Lens: Travel Poems*, available through Write Wing Publishing.

Michael Colonnese lives in Fayetteville, NC, where he directs the Creative writing Program at Methodist University and serves as the managing editor of Longleaf Press. His latest book is a mystery novel entitled *Sex and Death, I Suppose.*

Barbara Crooker's work has appeared in journals such as*: Nimrod, The Green Mountains Review, The Valparaiso Poetry Review, South Carolina Review, Tar River Review,* and anthologies, such as *The Bedford Introduction to Literature.* Her books are *Radiance*, winner of the Word Press First Book Award (2005) and finalist for the 2006 Paterson Poetry Prize; *Line Dance,* winner of the 2009 Paterson Award for Literary Excellence; *More* (C&R Press, 2010); and *Gold* (the Poeima Poetry Series, Cascade Books, 2013).

Barbara Duffey is an assistant professor of English at Dakota Wesleyan University. Her poetry has appeared in Prairie Schooner, Best New Poets 2009, The Indiana Review, and elsewhere. She has published creative non-fiction in CutBank and has a short story forthcoming in the Exigencies anthology from Dark House Press. She lives in Mitchell, SD, with her husband and son.

Donna Decker is a writer and spoken word performer; former creative writing and current business communications professor; volunteer wildlife rescuer and sea turtle patroller; and avid public radio listener; and has recently completed a collection of essays on living near the Gulf. Her recent CD, *I Have Your Petty Secret,* is a collaborative work of spoken word and music. She has widely published her poetry and essays in places such as *Between Two Rivers Anthology: Stories from the Red Hills to the Gulf* and Tallahassee's *Apalachee Review*. She listens to and is a member of WFSU 88.9 FM out of Tallahassee, Florida. Her website is *donnadecker.net.*

Blas Falconer is the author of *The Foundling Wheel* (Four Way Books 2012) and *A Question of Gravity and Light* (University of Arizona Press 2007). The recipient of an NEA Fellowship, the Maureen Egen Writers Exchange, and a Tennessee Individual Artist Grant, his poems have been featured by *Poets and Writers*, The Poetry Foundation, and Poetry Society of America. A coeditor of *Mentor and Muse: Essays from Poets to Poets* (Southern Illinois University Press 2010) and *The Other Latino: Writing Against a Singular Identity* (University of Arizona Press 2011), he teaches at the University of Southern California and in the low-residency MFA at Murray State University

Rupert Fike's collection of poems, *Lotus Buffet (Brick Road Poetry Press)* was named Finalist in the 2011 Georgia Author of the Year Awards. He has been nominated for Pushcart prizes in fiction and poetry with work appearing in *The Southern Review of Poetry, Rosebud, Natural Bridge, The Georgetown Review, A & U America's AIDS Magazine, The Atlanta Review* and others. He has a poem inscribed in a downtown Atlanta plaza, and his non-fiction, *Voices from The Farm,* is now in its second printing with accounts of life on a spiritual commune in the 1970s.

Jennifer Flescher's poems have been published in Fulcrum, LIT, The Harvard Review and the blog for Best American Poetry, as well as others. They have appeared in two anthologies, *Chopin with Cherries* (Moonrise Press, 2010) and *City of Big Shoulders* (University of Iowa Press, 2012). She has been nominated for Best New Poets and the Pushcart Prize and is the editor and publisher of *Tuesday; An Art Project*.

Deborah Gang's creative non-fiction and poetry have been published in *Literarymama*, and her poems have been seen in *J Journal/CUNY, New Verse News, The Michigan Poet* and *The Healing Muse/SUNY*.

Howie Good, a journalism professor at SUNY New Paltz, is the author of the forthcoming poetry collection *The Middle of Nowhere* (Olivia Eden Publishing), as well as numerous other books, including *Echo's Bones* and *Danger Falling Debris* (Red Bird Chapbooks). He co-edits White Knuckle Press with Dale Wisely. He listens to WAMC.

Richard Hamwi was born and raised in Los Angeles and received his Masters of Fine Arts from the University of California, Irvine. He currently teaches English at California State University at Long Beach.

Kenneth Hart teaches Writing at NYU. His poems have been published in *Arts and Letters, Mississipi Review, North American Review, Barrow Street, The Bellingham Review, Poet Lore,* and elsewhere. His book reviews appear regularly in *The Journal of New Jersey Poets*. He is the 2007 co-winner of the Allen Ginsberg Award, and the recipient of the 2008 editor's prize for *New Ohio Review*. His poem "Keep America Beautiful" was read by Garrison Keillor on *The Writer's Almanac* in 2009. His book *Uh Oh Time,* was selected by Mark Jarman as winner of the 2007 Anhinga Prize for poetry.

M.E. Hope's publications include: *Rattle; The Oregonian; High Desert Journal; Hubbub; Jefferson Monthly; The Fairfield Review; The Muses' Handprint; WORM 39; Soundzine;*

Cloudbank; Bellowing Ark; Prairie Poetry; Moving Mountain; Thresholds; Oregon Literary Review; Literary Bohemian; OutwardLink.net. And anthologies: *Verseweavers; New Poets of the American West; Alsop's Review 1; What the River Brings, Oregon River Poems; These Mountains that Separate Us; Try to Have Your Writing Make Sense;* and *Proud to Be: Writing by American Warriors, Volume 2.* Her chapbook *The Past is Clean* was published in 2010 by Uttered Chaos Press, Eugene Oregon

Juleigh Howard-Hobson's writing has appeared in such places as *The First Line, HipMama, The Found Poetry Review, & The Barefoot Muse.* Her work has been nominated for both "The Best of the Net" and The Pushcart Prize.

Kate Hutchinson teaches English and is Fine Arts Coordinator at a public high school in suburban Chicago. A chapbook of her poetry, *The Gray Limbo of Perhaps*, was published in summer, 2012, by Finishing Line Press. Her poems have appeared in dozens of literary magazines, and she is a Pushcart nominee. Kate blogs at "Life on Both Sides of the Window" (*poetkatehutchinson.word press.com*).

Luisa A. Igloria is the author of *Ode to the Heart Smaller than a Pencil Eraser* (selected by Mark Doty for the 2014 May Swenson Award, forthcoming from Utah State University Press in summer 2014); *Night Willow* (Phoenicia Publishing, spring 2014); *The Saints of Streets* (University of Santo Tomas Publishing House, 2013); *Juan Luna's Revolver* (University of Notre Dame Press, 2009 Ernest Sandeen Prize); *Trill & Mordent* (WordTech Editions, 2005); and eight other books. Originally from Baguio City, she teaches on the faculty of Old Dominion University where she currently directs the M.F.A. creative writing program. Her website is *www.luisaigloria.com*.

Tim Kahl *http://www.timkahl.com* is the author of *Possessing Yourself* (CW Books, 2009) and *The Century of Travel* (CW Books, 2012). His work has been published in *Prairie Schooner, Indiana Review, Ninth Letter, Notre Dame Review, The Journal, Parthenon West Review,* and many other journals in the U.S. He appears as Victor Schnickelfritz at the poetry and poetics blog *The Great American Pinup* (*http://greatamericanpinup.wordpress.com/*) and the poetry video blog *Linebreak Studios* [*http://linebreakstudios.blogspot.com/*]. He is also editor of Bald Trickster Press and *Clade Song* [*http://www.cladesong.com*]. He is the vice president and events coordinator of The Sacramento Poetry Center. He currently houses his father's literary estate—one volume: Robert Gerstmann's book of photos of Chile, 1932)

Marie Kane's poetry is widely published and anthologized. She was diagnosed with relapsing-remitting multiple sclerosis in 1991, and secondary-progressive MS in 2005. Her book, *Survivors in the Garden* (Big Table Publishing), which centers on her life with MS, was released in 2012 and chosen by the publisher for a Chapbook Pushcart Prize. She is the 2006 Bucks County Poet Laureate and a contributing editor for *Pentimento Magazine*. She lives in Yardley, PA, with her husband, Stephen Millner, an artist and listens to NPR on WHYY, Philadelphia.

Deda Kavanagh is one of eleven children, and grew up in suburban Detroit and lives in Bucks County Pennsylvania, where she listens to WHYY, Philadelphia. Her poems have appeared in *Paterson Literary Review, Schuylkill Valley Journal, U.S. 1 Worksheets, a*nd many other places. Her chapbook, *Bicycle Through a Covered Bridge*, was recently published by Finishing Line Press.

Elizabeth Kerlikowske is the author of two books and four chapbooks. She is the recent winner of the Standing Rock Cultural Arts Chapbook Contest. Her work appears in many publications including Poemeleon, Cincinnati Review, Slab, and The Binnacle. Kerlikowske is also president of the nonprofit Friends of Poetry, an organization dedicated to promoting poetry in southwest Michigan.

Kathryn A. Kopple is a specialist in Latin American literature (NYU, Ph.D.) Her poetry and prose can be found in the 2012 Fall Issue of *The Threepenny Review, Construction Lit Mag, Philadelphia Stories, Sleet, The Hummingbird Review, Danse Macabre, Metropolis, Contemporary Haibun Online, Haydens*

Ferry Review blog, *Lakeview International Journal of Literature and Art*, *100 Word Story* (forthcoming), *Bellevue Literary Review* (Fragile Environments Issue, 2014), among other publications. She is a regular contributor to Unusual Historicals, a blog devoted to historical fiction. She is also the author of *Little Velásquez* (Mirth Press, 2012), a novel set in 15th century Spain.

Judy Kronenfeld's most recent collections of poetry are *Shimmer* (WordTech Editions, 2012) and the second edition of *Light Lowering in Diminished Sevenths*, winner of the 2007 Litchfield Review Poetry Book Prize (Antrim House, 2012). Her poems have appeared in many print and online journals such as *Calyx, Cimarron Review, The American Poetry Journal, Natural Bridge, Poetry International, Spoon River Poetry Review, Women's Review of Books,* and *The Pedestal;* two dozen poems have appeared in anthologies such as *Before There Is Nowhere to Stand: Palestine/Israel: Poets Respond to the Struggle*(Lost Horse, 2012), and *Beyond Forgetting: Poetry and Prose about Alzheimer's Disease* (Kent State, 2009). She is Lecturer Emerita, Creative Writing Dept., UC Riverside, and Associate Editor of the online poetry journal, *Poemeleon.* Visit her website at *http://judykronenfeld.com.*

Jane Rosenberg LaForge is the author of *With Apologies to Mick Jagger, Other Gods, and All Women"* (The Aldrich Press 2012) and three chapbooks of poetry, including *The Navigation of Loss*, one of three winners of the Red Ochre Press 2012 chapbook competition. My experimental novel and memoir, *An Unsuitable Princess*, will be published by Jaded Ibis Press in 2014.

Ron.Lavalette lives in Vermont, land of the fur-bearing lake-trout, and has been widely published, both in print and online. A reasonable sample of his work can be found at EGGS OVER TOKYO *http://eggsovertokyo.blogspot.com*

Amy MacLennan has been published in *Hayden's Ferry Review, River Styx, Linebreak, Cimarron Review, Painted Bride Quarterly, Folio, and Rattle.* Her chapbook, *The Fragile Day,* was released from Spire Press in 2011, and her chapbook, *Weathering*, was published by Uttered Chaos Press in 2012.

Christina Lovin is the author of two full-length volumes of poetry—*ECHO* (Bottom Dog Press) and *A Stirring in the Dark* (Old Seventy Creek Press)—as well as three Finishing Line Press chapbooks *What We Burned for Warmth, Little Fires,* & *Flesh*. Her award-winning writing is widely published & anthologized, and has been supported by Elizabeth George Foundation, Kentucky Foundation for Women, and Kentucky Arts Council. She lives in Kentucky where she collects wool, dust, rejection letters, & shelter dogs. She is a lecturer in the English & Theatre Department at Eastern Kentucky University.

Joan Mazza has worked as a medical microbiologist, psychotherapist, seminar leader, and has been a Pushcart Prize nominee. Author of six books, including *Dreaming Your Real Self*(Penguin/Putnam), her poetry has appeared in *Rattle, Off the Coast, Kestrel, Slipstream, American Journal of Nursing, The MacGuffin, Mezzo Cammin, Buddhist Poetry Review*, and *The Nation*. She ran away from the hurricanes of South Florida to be surprised by the earthquakes and tornadoes of rural central Virginia, where she writes poetry and does fabric and paper art. www.JoanMazza.com

Kelly Nelson is the author of the chapbook *Rivers I Don't Live By* (Concrete Wolf, 2014). Her poetry has appeared in *2 River View, Mixed Fruit, Paddlefish, Dash, Eclectica* and elsewhere, and has been nominated for a Pushcart Prize. She is the recipient of a grant from the Arizona Commission on the Arts and the winner of Found Poetry Review's Dog-Ear Poetry Contest. She holds a PhD in Anthropology from Brandeis University, teaches Interdisciplinary Studies at Arizona State University and listens to NPR on KJZZ.

Richard Nester is the author of a forthcoming collection of poetry, *Buffalo Laughter* (Aldrich Press, 2014). He distrusts the liberal media but enjoys *Car Talk*. Go figure. His wife pestered him into writing this poem.

Robbi Nester is the editor of this anthology, assisted by Lavina Blossom. She is the author of a chapbook, *Balance (White Vio-*

let, 2012). Her collection of poetry, *A Likely Story,* will be published by Moon Tide Press this summer. She listens to KPCC FM, in Santa Monica, and watches public television on channels KOCE, in Huntington Beach, CA. and KCET, in Los Angeles.

Barbra Nightingale has had poems published in numerous poetry journals and anthologies, including *Southern Women Review*, *Rattle, The Sacramento Poetry Review*, *The Kansas Quarterly, The Missouri Review Online, InterlitQ, The Eloquent Athiest, Many Mountains Moving, Narrative Magazine* and *City of Big Shoulders*. Her most recent chapbook, *Two Voices, One Past* was a Runner Up in the 2010 Yellow Jacket Press Chapbook Award, and was published in September, 2010. *Geometry of Dreams* (2009) a full-length collection of poetry was published in 2009 *by* Word Tech Press, Ohio. She has six other collections of poetry, and a yet unpublished memoir, Ex-*Husbands and Other Strangers*.

Hal O'Leary is an 88 year-old Secular Humanist who believes that it is only through the arts that one is afforded an occasional glimpse into the otherwise incomprehensible. He began his writing career upon retiring from a life in the theatre at age eighty-four and has now been published in fifteen different countries. Hal is the recipient of an Honorary Doctor of Humane Letters from West Liberty University. It is his only degree, having been a drop-out from the same institution sixty-four years earlier.

Susan Blackwell Ramsey's book *A Mind Like This* was published in 2012 by the University of Nebraska Press. She lives in Kalamazoo, Michigan.

Penelope Scrambly Schott's most recent books are *Lovesong for Durfur*, a tribute to a small wheat growing town in central Oregon, and *Lillie Was a Goddess, :illie Was a Whore,* a verse study of prostitution.

Brittney Scott received her MFA from Hollins University. She was the 2012 recipient of the Joy Harjo Poetry Prize and the Dorothy Sargent Rosenberg Poetry Prize. Her poems have appeared or are forthcoming in such journals as *Prairie Schooner, The New Republic, Crab Orchard Review, Poet Lore, New South, Notre Dame Review, The Malahat Review, Water~Stone Review, Cold Mountain Review, Salamander, Folio, Copper Nickel, The Journal, KNOCK, Jabberwock Review, Basalt,* and *Quiddity*.

Patricia L. Scruggs is a Southern Californian by way of Colorado and Alberta, Canada. A retired high school art teacher, her work has appeared in *Cultural Weekly, CALYX, ONTHEBUS, Spillway, RATTLE,* and *Qarrtsiluni,* as well as the anthologies *13 Los Angeles Poets, Deliver Me, So Luminous the Wildflowers* and *LUMMOX II.*

Martha Silano is the author of four books of poetry: *What the Truth Tastes Like, Blue Positive, The Little Office of the Immaculate Conception,* and *Reckless Lovely*. She also co-edited, with Kelli Russell Agodon, *The Daily Poet: Day-By-Day Prompts For Your Writing Practice* (Two Sylvias Press 2013). Her poems have appeared in *Paris Review, North American Review,* where she won the 2014 James Hearst Poetry Prize, *American Poetry Review,* and elsewhere, and have appeared in over two-dozen anthologies, including *American Poetry: The Next Generation* and *The Best American Poetry 2009*. She has earned fellowships and grants from the University of Arizona Poetry Center, Washington State Artist Trust, Washington 4Culture, and Seattle Arts Commission, among others. Martha edits *Crab Creek Review*, curates Beacon Bards, a monthly poetry reading series, and teaches at Bellevue College.

M. E. Silverman is editor and founder of *Blue Lyra Review* and Review Editor of *Museum of Americana*. He is on the board of *32 Poems*. His chapbook, *The Breath before Birds Fly* (ELJ Press, 2013), is available. His poems have appeared in over 70 journals, including: *Crab Orchard Review, 32 Poems, December,* Chicago *Quarterly Review,* North*Chicago Review, Hawai'iPacific Review, I-70 Review, The Southern Poetry Anthology, The Los Angeles Review, Mizmor L'David Anthology: The Shoah, Neon, Many Mountains Moving, Pacific Review, Because I Said So Anthology* and other magazines.

He recently completed editing a contemporary Jewish anthology with Deborah Ager from Bloomsbury and is working on a second one.

Susan Snowden's work has appeared in numerous anthologies and literary journals, including *New Orleans Review, Aries, Pisgah Review, Emrys Journal,* and *moonShine review.* She has received awards from *Writer's Digest* magazine, Appalachian Writers' Association, NC Writers Network, and others. Her novel *Southern Fried Lies* won a 2013 IPPY Award for Best Fiction, Southeast Region. Susan lives in western North Carolina.

Nina Soifer is a free-lance food-writer from Northfield, NJ. Her poems have appeared in *The Literary Review, Alimentum-The Literature of Food, Small Batch, Thema, Mudfish* and other publications. She listens to WHYY Philadelphia.

Onna Solomon's writing has appeared in *Beloit Poetry Journal, Denver Quarterly, Cimarron Review,* and *32 Poems,* among others. She received her Master's in creative writing from Boston University, and now lives and works in Ann Arbor, MI, where she listens to 91.7 FM, WUOM.

Robin Stratton is a writing coach in the Boston area, and author of three novels and two chapbooks. She is Acquisitions Editor for Big Table Publishing Company and Senior Editor of *Boston Literary Magazine*. She'd love to have you visit her at www.robinstratton.com

Lisa Gluskin Stonestreet's *Tulips, Water, Ash* was selected for the Morse Poetry Prize and published by University Press of New England. Her poems have been awarded a Javits fellowship and a Phelan Award, and have appeared in journals and anthologies such as *Quarterly West, Blackbird, The Iowa Review, 32 Poems, Best New Poets,* and *The Bloomsbury Anthology of Contemporary Jewish American Poetry.*

Meryl Stratford is a retired teacher living in Hallandale Beach, Florida. Her poems have appeared in various magazines, and her chapbook, *The Magician's Daughter*, won the 2013 Yellow Jacket Press competition.

Recent books by **Marly Youmans** are: *Glimmerglass* (a novel from Mercer University Press, 2014); *Thaliad* (an adventure in blank verse from Phoenicia Publishing of Montreal); *The Foliate Head* (a collection of poems from UK's Stanza Press, currently in second printing); and *A Death at the White Camellia Orphanage* (winner of The Ferrol Sams Award in Fiction and the Silver Award in Fiction from *ForeWord*'s Book of the Year Awards.) Marly's NPR stations are WSKG in Binghamton, New York, where she has appeared several times on Bill Jaker's *Off the Page*, and WAMC in Albany.

After a lifetime of teaching at Salisbury University and raising a family, **Kit Zak** and her husband have moved to Lewes, DE. She has spent retirement involved in environmental activities, writing poetry, and visiting far-flung grandchildren. Her poems have been published in *The Broadhill Review, Avocet: A Journal of Nature Writing, The Blue Collar Review,* and *Newsversenews.*

The Liberal Media Made Me Do It

About The LUMMOX Press

LUMMOX Press was created in 1994 by RD Armstrong. It began as a self-publishing/DIY imprint for poetry by RD, aka Raindog. Several chapbooks were published and in late 1995 LUMMOX began publishing *The LUMMOX Journal*, a monthly small/underground press lit-arts mag. Available primarily by subscription, the *LJ* continued its exploration of the "creative process" until its demise as a print mag in 2006. It was hailed as one of the best monthlies in the small press by John Berbrich and Todd Moore.

In 1998, LUMMOX began publishing the Little Red Book series, and continues to do so, sporadically, today. To date there are some 60 titles in the series and a collection of poems from the first decade of the series has been published under the title, **The Long Way Home** (2009); it's a great way to explore the series.

Together with Chris Yeseta (Layout and Art Direction since 1997), RD continues to publish books that are both striking in their looks as well as their content…published because of the merit of the work, not the fame of the author. That's why there are so many first full-length collections in the roster (look for the *).

* * *

The following books are available directly from the LUMMOX Press via its website: *www.lummoxpress.com/lc/* or at LUMMOX c/o PO Box 5301, San Pedro, CA 90733. There are also E-Copy (PDF) versions of most titles available. Books with the letters SPD are also carried by Small Press Distribution.

The Wren Notebook by Rick Smith (2000)

Last Call: The Legacy of Charles Bukowski edited by RD Armstrong (2004)

On/Off the Beaten Path by RD Armstrong (2008)

Fire and Rain—Selected Poems 1993-2007 Volumes 1 & 2 by RD Armstrong (2008)*

El Pagano and Other Twisted Tales by RD Armstrong (short stories – 2008)*

New and Selected Poems by John Yamrus (2009)

The Riddle of the Wooden Gun by Todd Moore (2009)

Sea Trails by Pris Campbell (2009)
Down This Crooked Road—Modern Poetry from the Road Less Traveled
 edited by RD Armstrong and William Taylor, Jr. (2009)
Drive By by John Bennett (2010)
Modest Aspirations by Gerald Locklin & Beth Wilson (2010)
Steel Valley by Michael Adams (2010)*
Hard Landing by Rick Smith (2010)
A Love Letter to Darwin by Jane Crown (2010)*
E/OR—Living Amongst the Mangled by RD Armstrong (2010)
Ginger, Lily & Sweet Fire by H. Lamar Thomas (2010)*
Whose Cries Are Not Music by Linda Benninghoff (2011)*
Dog Whistle Politics by Michael Paul (2011)*
What Looks Like an Elephant by Edward Nudleman (2011)* SPD
Working the Wreckage of the American Poem edited by
 RD Armstrong (2011)
Living Among the Mangled (revised) by RD Armstrong,
 special edition, (2011)
The Accidental Navigator by Henry Denander (2011)
Catalina by Laurie Soriano (2011)* SPD
Born to Be Blue by Tony Moffeit (2011)
Last Call: the Bukowski Legacy Continues edited by
 RD Armstrong (2011)
Strong As Silk by Brigit Truex (2012)* SPD
The Instrument of Others by Leonard J. Cirino (2012)
If It We by Lisa Zaran (2012)*
The Names of Lost Things by Jason Hardung (2012)
Because, Just Because by Philip Ramp (2012)
Crazy Bone by Billy Jones (2012)
LUMMOX Magazine edited by RD Armstrong
 (see description below – 2012)
5150—A Memoir by Dana Christensen (2013)*
I See Hunger's Children by normal (2013)*

her by j/j hastain (2013)*

How Long the Night Is by Christine DeSimone (2013)

Songs of the Glue Machines by Nicolas Belardes (2013)

Breaking and Entering by D. R. Wagner (2013)

Me First by Ann Curran (2013)

What the Wind Says by Taylor Graham (2013)

Birth Mother Mercy by Alex Frankel (2013)

Broken Lines—The Art & Craft of Poetry by Judith Skillman (2013)

LUMMOX #2 edited by RD Armstrong (2013)

Whispering in a Mad Dog's Ear by Rick Smith (2014)

Wildwood by Kyle Laws (2014)

The Liberal Media Made Me Do It! edited by Robbi Nester (2014)

Once You Start Eating, You Will Never Stop by Tim Peeler (2014)

Pleasure in a Stained Universe by Norman Olson (2014)*

* * *

LUMMOX (the anthology) is a yearly print anthology (begun in 2012). It contains interviews, essays, articles, reviews, artwork, ads and lots of poetry (future issues will also feature special flashbacks to the old *LUMMOX Journal* archives). The focus of the first issue was FAVORITE POEMS, the theme for #2 was PLACE and for the third issue: DESIRE/ROAD KILL. Each issue features poetry from around the world.

LUMMOX is available by annual subscription for $25 USA and $35 WORLD. Visit *http://www.lummoxpress.com/lc/lummox-anthology-2/* for details.

www.ingramcontent.com/pod-product-compliance
Lightning Source LLC
Chambersburg PA
CBHW071209160426
43196CB00011B/2237